RESTORING
A HOUSE IN THE CITY

RESTORING
A HOUSE IN THE CITY

INGRID ABRAMOVITCH

PHOTOGRAPHS BY BRIAN PARK

ARTISAN | NEW YORK

FRONTISPIECE: A work on paper by the Dutch artist Hannah van Bart hangs in the entry to a vibrant turquoise bedroom in Brooklyn Heights (see Skyline View, page 195).

PHOTO CREDITS: Paul Costello (Charleston Revival), pp. 8, 9, 20, 22, 23, 24 (left); Thibault Jeanson (Star Turn), pp. 57, 58–59, 60, 64; Jason Schmidt (Bricks and Glass), pp. 5, 255, 261 (bottom).

Published by Artisan
A Division of Workman Publishing Company, Inc.
225 Varick Street
New York, NY 10014-4381
www.artisanbooks.com

Library of Congress Cataloging-in-Publication Data

Abramovitch, Ingrid.
    Restoring a house in the city / Ingrid Abramovitch.
            p. cm.
    Includes bibliographical references.
    ISBN 978-1-57965-350-7
    1.   Row houses—Conservation and restoration.   I. Title.

    NA7520.A27 2009
    728' .312—dc22   2009004411

Design by Jan Derevjanik and Stephanie Huntwork

Printed in Singapore
First printing, September 2009

10 9 8 7 6 5 4 3 2 1

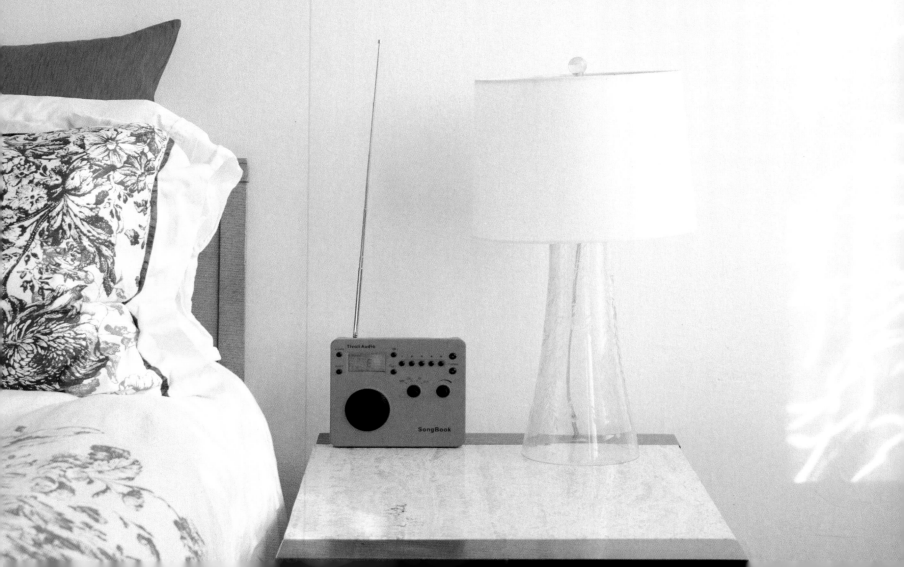

For my husband Joel,
my parents, Arlene and Henry,
and my two brownstone beauties,
Ruby and Lola.

"Where thou art, that is home."

—Emily Dickinson

CONTENTS

OPPOSITE: Philadelphia's Society Hill neighborhood has row houses dating to the 1700s.

PREFACE

In my first ten years as a student and young professional in New York, the city's legendary brownstones and classic town houses barely caught my eye. I was distracted by the sparkle of the more modern metropolis, commuting from a tenement apartment in the East Village to a series of magazine editing jobs in the glassy heart of midtown Manhattan. It took a dramatic lifestyle change—marriage and a baby—to change my perspective. Yes, for a Manhattanite I did the obvious: I packed up my belongings and decamped across the bridge to Brooklyn.

As we investigated real estate listings with a six-month-old in tow, my husband, Joel, shared his experiences of growing up in a Brooklyn brownstone in the 1970s. His father was an artist who wanted space at home for an art studio. The family moved to Boerum Hill, where mid-nineteenth-century town houses stood side by side with housing projects and a hulking nearby jail. The house they renovated, an 1850s Greek Revival, was an empty shell whose interior had been destroyed in a fire. It took another twenty years for Boerum Hill to become the neighborhood of his parents' dreams: a safe and lively enclave, filled with bookshops, cafes, and gourmet restaurants.

Ascending and descending the endless town house stairs, I was smitten by the homes' charmingly anachronistic grace notes, from the imposing classical entrances to the parlors straight out of Edith Wharton novels. Realtors pointed out such intriguing details as coffin corners, stair hall niches they said were designed for navigating Victorian coffins around tight turns (an urban myth, I later learned from Charles Lockwood's classic guide to New York

town houses, *Bricks and Brownstone*). Some of the homes we looked at were overly renovated (moldings and mantels were long gone, the facades sadly "modernized" with faux-brick), others were better preserved, but we couldn't imagine occupying their dark and narrow rooms. Still others retained original features like parquet floors and chandeliers barely noticeable under decades' worth of grime. The house we chose was a bay-windowed duplex in an Italianate brownstone on a sunny corner in Carroll Gardens, a leafy Italian-American neighborhood—and the setting for the movie *Moonstruck*—that was becoming a favorite of young families and professionals. Our apartment, while far from grand, nevertheless had a working fireplace, tin ceilings, and pine plank floors.

I quickly learned that in Brooklyn, the conversation always comes around to the topic of old houses—how to find one, how to live in one, how to cope with its endless quirks. There were entire blogs, such as Brownstoner, devoted to the topic of restoring old houses—and similar conversations were occurring in other cities, from Montreal to San Francisco, where urbanites were trying to bring historic houses back to life. How do you know whether an old house is for you? How do you hire an architect and a contractor? What's the best way to restore old windows? Is the chimney safe for lighting fires? This quest for information—and real-life inspiration from those who have been there and lived to tell the tale—inspired *Restoring a House in the City*, a contemporary guide to classic town house renovation.

INTRODUCTION

Buying an old house in the city is an act of bravery or faith—or at the very least, a step into the unknown. It begins like a romance: we're charmed by the high-ceilinged parlors and hand-crafted woodwork, and seduced by the luxury of having our own street entrance and the chance to have a garden in the midst of urban bustle. But then the inspector report arrives and our heart sinks. The roof leaks, the floors lean, the chimney flues need relining, and an ominous crack has been discovered in the stair hall. We ask ourselves: Will our wallets (and our marriages) survive the renovation? What of the constant care and nurturing that a century-plus house requires? Just what are we getting ourselves in for?

Restoring a House in the City is a book for the new generation of homeowners. We are the post-post-preservationists—renovation's third wave, a group that has rejected suburban flight for the chance to roost in the cosmopolitan city. We cherish our creaking old town houses and the amazing fact of their continued existence, and appreciate the efforts of architectural preservationists who have fought for decades to save landmark neighborhoods from the wrecking ball. As today's stewards, we want to do right by our houses. But at the same time we don't want to live in a museum. Leave the heavy draperies and drawing rooms to the Victorians: we want efficient kitchens in homes that once housed live-in servants and modern bathrooms where indoor plumbing was once a luxury. It can be challenging to strike the right balance between old and new. But as the renovations featured in this book show, an antique home can be surprisingly adaptable.

The book features twenty-one homeowners, in ten cities and towns in the United States and Canada, who have taken the great leap of purchasing and restoring an antique dwelling. Though the information in the book is meant to be helpful for anyone who lives in a pre–World War II apartment or home, the central focus is on the classic town houses, row houses, and brownstones that line so many residential neighborhoods.

By a **town house,** I am referring to a three-to-six story home, attached or detached, whose vertical layout and small footprint has its origins in Europe, where the style has existed since medieval times. A town house has a formal first floor, deriving from Venetian palazzos, where the *piano nobile,* or principal floor, was situated above ground to protect fine furnishings from water damage. A **row house** is

a townhouse whose facade is attached to and nearly identical to its neighbors. This architectural device, popularized in Georgian England, was an attempt to create city blocks with the harmonious appearance of a palace front. Today, the term *row house* usually refers to the small, adjoined homes originally built for working-class families. Meanwhile, in New York, the town house is commonly referred to as a **brownstone,** whether or not its facade is swathed in the chocolate-hued sandstone that was all the rage in the city in the nineteenth century.

The homeowners in *Restoring a House in the City* are as diverse as their homes. Among their ranks are a pair of Baltimore set designers, architects and interior designers, a photographer, two fashion designers, a movie-set veteran married to a twelfth-generation Charlestonian, and the actress Julianne Moore. Moore and her husband, the movie director Bart Freundlich, searched for years for a New York town house before finding just the right one in Greenwich Village, and overseeing every aspect of its renovation. "If you are really serious about renovating an old house," she said, "try to live in it first, and figure out *how* you want to live in it."

The houses in the book span 160 years. In Philadelphia, a young couple with a taste for modern furnishings renovates a 1763 Colonial. In San Francisco, two Williams-Sonoma executives bring a cobwebby 1920 Edwardian town house back to life. There are modest homes, and almost mansions, period pieces (where every detail has been thoroughly researched and preserved), and town houses where the entire back walls have been replaced with sheets of glass.

Yet while each approach is unique, the twenty-one renovation stories have much in common. In every case, homeowners discovered the ins and outs of overhauling an old building, assembling teams of architects, contractors, and artisans, and getting up to speed on the latest research on restoring bricks and mortar. They became conversant in the quaint and highly specific vocabulary of restoration, learning the difference between crown molding and corbels, medallions and modillians. Most challenging of all, they survived lengthy renovations whose constant fluctuations would give anyone vertigo.

Even the best-planned old-house renovations are stressful. Structural flaws have a way of appearing midway through a project. Contractors have a habit of disappearing. Architects grapple with the perennial challenge of bringing light into dark town house interiors. Whatever the budget, the money always seems to run out. And yet renovation survivors seem to fall into two categories: those who love their homes and never want to leave them, and those who enjoy the process so much that, when the work is finally done, they're already eyeing that fixer-upper down the block.

There is much talk nowadays about sustainable architecture, certainly a worthwhile cause. Many homeowners are trying to renovate their old houses using ecologically sound materials and methods, from low-VOC paints and energy-efficient appliances to solar power panels on the roof. While commendable, it's worth noting that restoring an antique home—especially one within walking distance of public transportation—is an inherently green act. With the proper care, a house that has survived for a century or longer could easily last another hundred and fifty years.

Of course, it's not the past or the future that preoccupies most old-home remodelers: it's what they want for the present. It's creating the perfect house for the here and now. "It's worth the temporary trouble and pain," said a woman who spent three years renovating her brownstone. "You will have a lifetime to enjoy."

—Ingrid Abramovitch

PREVIOUS SPREAD, LEFT: The parlor of a historic brownstone in Brooklyn Heights (see Skyline View, page 195) feels contemporary with its modern art, zebra-patterned curtains, and backgammon table.
OPPOSITE: In Charleston (top left), a new raised swimming pool adds a modern counterpoint to the back garden of an 1843 town home with an attached kitchen house (see Charleston Revival, page 21); a wall of Victorian built-in cabinets (top right) was retrofitted with lighting and glass shelves and now serves as the stylish backdrop to a modern open kitchen (see All in the Family, page 183); and an antique console mirror (below) reflects the ornate plaster moldings of an Italianate town house in Troy, New York (see Forgotten Grandeur, page 43). ABOVE LEFT: In Greenwich Village, the sleek new roof level of a Greek Revival town house has indoor and outdoor terraces and a view of neighboring rooftops (see Bricks and Glass, page 253). ABOVE: Built before indoor plumbing, a Federal-style row house has a tiny bathroom that was added at a later date and squeezed onto a stair landing (see Simply French, page 133).

A GUIDE TO TOWN HOUSE STYLES

COLONIAL | 1700–1780 |
Narrow widths and hand-crafted features

A Colonial town house is a chance to step into history: whether a Philadelphia row home older than the Revolution, or a Baltimore alley house that might once have been the residence of oyster-shuckers or freed slaves. These eighteenth-century gems owe a debt to Georgian London, where the taste in cities was for a house with a private entrance. Builders tried to squeeze as many Colonials as possible onto one street: the result was the elongated row home. These houses still exist in such cities as Philadelphia (see Minimalonialism, page 213) and Alexandria, Virginia, and are beloved for their handsome details, including facades in locally made brick, external shutters, and twelve-over-twelve paned windows. But those who like living large should look elsewhere: with average widths of twelve to sixteen feet, the Colonial town house is the anti-McMansion.

FEDERAL | 1780–1830 |
Neoclassical geometry and subtle details

The Federal style, also known as the Adam style after the Scottish architects and brothers Robert and James Adam, is the house type of choice for those who love classical proportions. Influenced by the Renaissance Italian architect Andrea Palladio, the Adams created in their native England blocks of residences that were designed to work together as one grand composition. In America, Boston's Charles Bulfinch assumed the Adams's mantle. Though usually not more than four stories high Federal houses were wider than Colonials: the average width in New York City was twenty-five feet. Fans of the style extol its neat geometry of square rooms and six-over-six sash windows that let in plenty of natural light. The charming facades, either in wood shingle or brick, have understated flourishes such as arched windows, dentils, cornices, and wrought-iron railings—and help make Greenwich Village one of New York's most desirable neighborhoods (see The Federalist, page 13).

GREEK REVIVAL | 1830–1860 |
Classical motifs and statement-making parlors

For a young nation in search of an architectural vocabulary, Athens—the birthplace of democracy—spoke the loudest. As town houses grew ever taller, their exteriors became increasingly decked with ancient Greek features, from columns to capitals. Flat rooflines and austere masonry facades balance formal front entrances, where stairs ascend to stoops and front doors are flanked by pilasters. Three full stories high, these houses also have a sunken ground floor, known as a basement, where the kitchen and family dining room were originally located. The soaring parlor rooms, often with fourteen-foot ceilings, are brightened by daylight that streams in through double-hung windows, made possible by a nineteenth-century invention—factory glass. Contemporary fans of the style include the actress Julianne Moore (see Star Turn, page 57) and homeowners in Boston (see The Brahmin, page 35), Brooklyn (see Skyline View and Light Box, pages 195 and 239), and the South (see Charleston Revival, page 21; Straight and Narrow, page 79; and Ghost Story, page 147).

ITALIANATE |1840–1870|
Embellished facades and wedding-cake moldings

Hugely popular in their time, Italianate style town houses came in a variety of facades, from brick to stucco, and can still be found in cities as varied as Chicago, New Orleans, and Troy, New York (see Forgotten Grandeur, page 43). But for many, the form is synonymous with the classic New York brownstone (see The Nostalgic, page 67; Graphic Pop, page 225; All in the Family, page 183; and Soul Survivor, page 99). Based on Italian Renaissance palazzos, this highly ornamental style is decidedly showy, with its ornate cornices, marble fireplace mantels, ceiling rosettes, and intricate millwork. The Italianate house is more easily adapted to modern living than earlier period houses because many were built with luxury amenities of the time—bathrooms, running water, gas lighting, and central heating. Most are eighteen or twenty feet wide, but some are as narrow as fourteen or even twelve feet. Italianates compensate by being taller and deeper, but this poses the challenge of bringing light into the floor's windowless centers.

LATE VICTORIAN/EDWARDIAN |1860–1910|
Off-the-shelf architectural elements and lots of variety

While earlier town houses had distinct stylistic features, the late Victorian and Edwardian periods incorporated a variety of designs. The industrial revolution was in full swing, and everything from decorative detailing to roofs and doors could suddenly be mass-produced and shipped long distances on the railroads. The resulting availability of materials led to a new wave of architectural styles—such as Second Empire, Romanesque Revival, Queen Anne, and Neo-Grec—each with its own flourishes and quirks. Later, during King Edward VII's monarchy, architecture took on a more restrained appearance (see The Edwardian, page 111). More classical in porportion, Edwardian homes substituted light-filled rooms for darker Victorian layouts.

ECLECTIC |1901–1939|
Individuality and a range of architectural traditions

Up until the turn of the twentieth century, town houses were often built in rows by developers or builders. By 1901, wealthy city dwellers wanted something different: a house of their own. This need gave rise to the Eclectic movement, in which European-trained architects drew upon the full range of architectural tradition—from classical to medieval to modern. Today's town house buyer may need an architectural field guide to pinpoint any of the period's wide range of styles. Eclectic homes can range from the Parisian-influenced hauteur of a Beaux-Arts limestone (see Diplomatic Core, page 89), to such quirkier revivalist styles as a Tudor Gothic (see Canadian Gothic, page 123)—often all coexisting on the same block.

Restoring Tradition

TO TAKE UP RESIDENCE in a classic urban town house is to inhabit a living antique. Today, in an age of Sheetrock and instant gratification, the craftsmanship and materials that went into the construction of even the most modest of historic town houses would be prohibitive. Only the very ambitious (and well-funded) can support the team of artisans—carpenters; plasterers; brick masons; stone carvers; and craftsmen of doors, windows, and stairs—that would be needed to create a replica with the quality and detail of the originals. Some owners so cherish the dazzling workmanship in their homes that they dedicate themselves to careful stewardship of the past. For them, part of the fun is in playing detective, learning about prior occupants, and through research and observation, piecing together a history of the house and how it evolved through the generations.

In the pages that follow, we meet homeowners who have restored town houses from the brink of ruin—after many decades of decay and neglect—to the showpieces of their historic heyday. In Troy, New York, in a double-wide brownstone overlooking a lost-in-time nineteenth-century square, a priceless antique console is discovered lying in the carriage house under layers of dirt, then lovingly restored and returned to its rightful spot of honor in the main home's grand parlor. In Charleston, a Greek Revival town home is carefully taken apart, brick by brick, and reassembled under the expert oversight of Richard "Moby" Marks, one of the nation's top restoration contractors. An 1835 Beacon Hill town house in Boston gets the kind of lavish treatment—European fabrics, custom carpets, antiques, hand-painted murals—rarely seen since the style's peak in the nineteenth century. And a New York fashion mogul renovates one of the oldest row homes in Greenwich Village, taking care to preserve the crooked floors that contribute to its charm.

That all of these town houses today accommodate active contemporary households and modern amenities, from central air-conditioning to high-speed Internet connections, is proof that a preservationist mind-set has nothing to do with living in the past.

THE FEDERALIST

|GREENWICH VILLAGE, NEW YORK CITY|

Date built: 1836 | Width: 22 feet | Stories: 4 | Square footage: 2,700 | Bedrooms: 3 | Fireplaces: 3
Year purchased: 2002 | Length of renovation: 9 months | House style: Federal

In Greenwich Village, Manhattan's logical grid gives way to a neighborhood where the leafy streets have a quirkier layout. Some roads cross on a diagonal, others zigzag, and several curve: tiny Bedford Street is home to both the area's oldest row house, built in 1799, and its narrowest one, just nine and a half feet wide. Adding to the neighborhood's charm is one of the richest collections of landmarked town houses in the United States.

The Village's residents, like its streets, have long been rule breakers: this corner of New York has attracted artists and iconoclasts from Dylan Thomas to Bob Dylan. Lately it has become the chosen residence of a fashionable crowd, people like Robert Duffy, the longtime business partner of the fashion designer Marc Jacobs. In 2001, Duffy bought

a Federal town house in the heart of the Village, with black wood shutters and an iron railing flanked on either side of its entrance by acorn finials.

It is the shortest house on the block, as Duffy describes it to first-time visitors, and like many homes of its era it started out even smaller: after a fire destroyed part of the original house in 1893, a new living room was added circa 1910, and the dining room was tacked on in the 1970s. Compared with the showier brownstones in the neighborhood, with their fourteen-foot ceilings and elaborate parlors, Duffy's house is intimate. "I looked at so many town houses and they were all so intimidating," Duffy says. "This one is not grand. It felt manageable."

Architect Stephan Jaklitsch, who has worked with Duffy on the design of Marc Jacobs stores, oversaw the renovation. He researched Federal homes and set out to make this one more livable for his client while tampering as little as possible with its intact architecture. If that meant leaving crooked floors and holes in the floorboards, so be it. "Everything leans and I love that," Duffy says. "When you are in the basement, you look up and see light shining through the floorboards."

The decor, which Duffy developed with the help of interior designer James Mohn, is mutable. A passionate collector of everything from modern art to Asian decorative arts and art deco furniture, Duffy is constantly reworking what he displays. His varied art collection includes works by such artists as Mark Rothko and Milton Avery. The furnishings span the eighteenth, nineteenth, and twentieth centuries. In the library, for example, there are fine American antiques that Duffy inherited from his family, who lived outside of Pittsburgh. These include an Empire desk and vitrine and a grandfather clock, which coexist with a Regency table from Paris, where Duffy used to live, and a pair of English tufted armchairs reupholstered in navy leather.

There were a few alterations. A 1970s kitchen made way for a dramatic pine-paneled dining room with mirrors on all four walls, a space Duffy had always dreamed of having. Two of the upstairs rooms, which were particularly cozy, were combined to create a larger master bedroom suite. Still, this is not the tricked-out house one might

OPPOSITE: Duffy uses his home as a backdrop for his wide-ranging collection of art and ephemera. Here, a nineteenth-century black marble mantel showcases a Jack Pierson photograph, a wire sculpture, and a set of 1970s mugshots that he discovered in a junk shop. LEFT: The dining room's white pine paneling, which completely covers the walls and ceiling, looks antique but was added during the latest renovation. ABOVE: The adjacent galley kitchen is accessible through an invisible door that blends into the woodwork.

expect of a man who makes his living in fashion. There are few closets, for example, and the ones that exist are miniature. The kitchen is now a narrow galley adjacent to the dining room; for Duffy, who rarely cooks, it is more than enough space.

In 2001, Duffy had the idea of opening a Marc Jacobs store around the corner because he thought it would be fun to walk to work. He says the decision had unintended consequences, creating a real estate revolution in the neighborhood. The Bleecker Street store was so successful that the company soon added four more boutiques—two up the street and two more around the corner. Local businesses were soon supplanted by other luxury retailers as a once-quiet enclave was transformed almost overnight into a high-end shopping destination and tourist mecca.

But gentrification comes with the territory and Duffy isn't complaining. In truth, he is proud to have contributed to the restoration of his own Village block, which, while once down and out, has now returned to its original state: a tree-lined street of elegant town houses. "I loved bringing an old house back to life," he says, "back to what it was meant to be."

OPPOSITE: The spacious master bedroom suite. LEFT: The master bathroom's vintage fixtures are complemented by shutters that are antique looking but new. BELOW: A guest bedroom is decorated with toile wallpaper and an antique bed purchased in Savannah.

CHARLESTON REVIVAL

Date built: 1843 | Width: 48 feet | Stories: 4 | Square footage: 9,900 | Bedrooms: 7 | Fireplaces: 11 working
Year purchased: 2003 | Length of renovation: 4 years | House style: Greek Revival

In historic Charleston, Richard Marks is the contractor of choice, both for his expertise in bringing antique houses back from the brink, and for his detectivelike pursuit of their forgotten past. Marks, who goes by the nickname Moby, was the first person that Ozey and Sarah Horton called when they were thinking of buying one of Charleston's grandest town houses, the William C. Gatewood house. Situated on one of the oldest streets in town, the Gatewood is a classic Charleston side yard, named for its long two-story porch—known in Charleston as a piazza—that runs the length of the south side of the house and gives way to the garden in back. The purpose of the piazza is dual: to offer shade from sun during the stifling Charleston summers and a view of the lemon trees lining the long allée in the side yard.

ABOVE: The finishes in the kitchen house were left deliberately rustic in keeping with its early character—a "new" floor was laid in reclaimed Charleston brick from the early 1800s and the original staircase was restored. OPPOSITE: The open-plan kitchen—with its La Cornue range, sitting room with television, and state-of-the-art appliances concealed in built-in cabinetry—is the most contemporary modification to the town house. A dropped ceiling was removed to reveal the original framing while adding height to the space.

The Hortons—he is a tenth-generation Charlestonian and a management consultant, she is a former assistant director who has worked with Clint Eastwood and Tommy Lee Jones—are both passionate preservationists. Determined to resuscitate a local architectural gem, they searched for eight years for a house with enough original features to make a restoration worthwhile. Finally, they found the Gatewood house, a particularly fine and rare example of Greek Revival architecture for the area. The building had endured ten different owners, a major earthquake, and several decades as a rooming house. Still, its bones were remarkably intact, from the S-shaped newel post at the base of the main staircase to the lofty parlor rooms of the grand second floor, with their lavish ornamental plasterwork. What's more, there was an old kitchen house in the rear, which had been connected to the main house sometime after the Civil War. Unfortunately, Gatewood was not for sale. But the Hortons wrote to the owner explaining their intent to undertake a serious restoration, and their offer was accepted.

The Hortons's worst fear—that the house's foundation would need to be overhauled—was allayed by a structural report that deemed it stable. But everywhere else, the house was coming apart. Among the countless alarming discoveries, an inspection

RIGHT: For reasons of fire safety, the kitchen house, located at the rear of the property, was originally separate from the main house. The buildings were later adjoined after the Civil War. Architect Gil Schafer used the connecting passage to create a butler's pantry and bar, with brick walls (above) showing the exposed face of the original exterior structures. OPPOSITE: In the much grander main house, the hall was painted in Rhett Pumpkin, a shade from the Colors of Historic Charleston paint collection. The front parlor has classical American furniture from the first quarter of the nineteenth century, collected by the Hortons over the years.
FOLLOWING SPREAD: The dining room (left), which leads to the middle parlor (right), is decorated with hand-painted scenic wallpaper from de Gournay. The mahogany dining table was made in Boston in 1830, and the 1820s Klismos chairs are from Philadelphia.

revealed that the brick in the south walls had become delaminated as the mortar had deteriorated. The roof trusses were rotted, the parlor's ceiling joists were on the verge of collapse, and in one corner the house had sunk twelve inches, a probable consequence of the Charleston earthquake of 1886. Amazingly, the Hortons decided to proceed. They hired Marks to oversee the restoration, working in tandem with New York–based architect Gil Schafer, a former president of the Institute of Classical Architecture and Classical America, who was given the mandate of updating the house without compromising its historic value.

Marks, who teaches preservation at a local university and oversees a staff of fifty artisans, researchers, and experts, studied the house for five months. Schafer says it "felt as though we were living out a thrilling episode of *CSI: Charleston*. Moby and his team would tackle each element of the house with forensic focus—they were sleuths and archeologists, and best of all, they were creative problem solvers."

OPPOSITE: The parlor's triple-hung windows are original to the house. They were taken apart and restored using Thomas Jefferson's Monticello house as inspiration. The windows open to the floor and adjust to varying breezes. LEFT: The original pocket doors, cleaned and restored, separate the two parlor's and help keep rooms warm in winter.

The house was literally taken apart and put back together. Craig Bennett, a structural engineer, dismantled half of the disintegrating south wall, salvaging all of the original bricks and stitching the wall back up with thousands of stainless-steel tie rods. Two feet of soil were excavated below the house to create air circulation around the joists. On the north face of the house, the wall was pulling away from the internal central staircase and leaning into the neighboring alley. The solution was to reinforce the sagging steps with steel channels and flitch plates and, in a feat of engineering, to use the staircase itself as a thirty-two-foot brace to tie the wall back into the property.

Once satisfied that the house was not going to collapse, Marks located the building's original floor plan, chain of title, will, and probate records from local archives, discovering that Virginia-born Gatewood was a wealthy merchant of sea island cotton and rice who had six children, ten slaves, and a dog. This kind of information, along with checklists detailing Gatewood's furnishings, gives a sense of what the rooms looked like and what purposes they served. Marks also treated the house itself as an archaeological site, gathering "nail typologies," in which nail styles are used to determine the age of the home's architectural elements, and finding evidence that the house had such 1840s high luxuries as gas lighting and indoor plumbing.

Marks studies an old house for what he calls ghost marks—traces on walls that reveal the presence of features long removed. In the Hortons' house, he discovered evidence of a missing staircase, as well as clues that the kitchen house had once had an outside porch. The Hortons put them both back. Much attention was also paid to making the house look as much as possible as though it had not been touched since the 1840s. Extra layers of paint were applied to give surfaces an aged appearance. Outside, the brick's crumbling mortar was placed under a microscope, and its recipe—a mixture of crushed brick, feldspar, crushed stone, quartz, lime, and color—

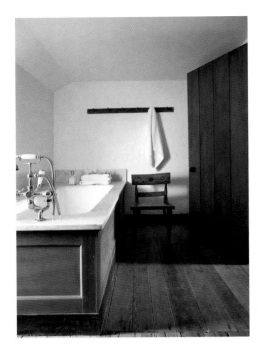

ABOVE: The design for the attic floor bathroom was inspired by Charleston's landmark Aiken-Rhett House. The paint color was matched to the shade of a plank-and-batten door found in the attic and now installed in the bath. The peg board is also original to the house. ABOVE RIGHT: This bedroom's American four-poster plantation bed from the 1840s belonged to Ozey Horton's grandfather. OPPOSITE: This bathroom in the kitchen house has walls of mill-sawn cypress, original to the house, when this room would have been used for dry goods storage. The lighting, fabricated by Marks, is designed to resemble traditional gas lamps from the Greek Revival period.

reconstituted. "When we leave a job, we don't want anyone to know we were there," Marks says.

Like many grand old houses, this one was originally designed to have two separate spheres: one for the servants, and one for the served. But the Hortons have no live-in staff and Sarah, an accomplished chef, loves to spend time in the kitchen. Schafer says his first impulse was to indulge the Hortons with such creature comforts as luxury bathrooms and large closets. Most of his East Coast clientele expect those kinds of modern amenities. But in Charleston, his ideas were received with extreme caution. "Everyone would look at me in horror and say: 'We don't tear down walls that have been here since 1840,'" he says. "I learned to ask Moby: 'Do they do this here?'"

Schafer ultimately devised several ingenious solutions using what he calls "smoke and mirrors": rather than locate a shower down the hall from a guest bedroom, as he found it, for example, he managed to conceal a full bathroom suite inside a white cabinet designed to look like an 1840s wardrobe armoire. Without moving a single wall or feature, he and Marks succeeded in updating the house with six new bathrooms, two new kitchens, three new staircases, modern heating, central air-conditioning, new electrical wiring, high-speed data lines, and an elevator. Each alteration was designed to be easily removable so that the fundamental integrity of the historic house remains unchanged.

In the end, the restoration of the Gatewood house took more than four years. The Hortons are still recuperating as they painstakingly assemble a collection of fine antiques worthy of their historic home. They take immense pride in salvaging one of the town's great houses and knowing that it will likely stand firm for another 150 years. "It was a privilege to restore the house and bring it back to life," Sarah says. "As we say in Charleston, we are just the stewards for the time being."

RESTORATION NOTES ENTRANCES

From pediments to columns, pilasters to raised panel doors, the workmanship and detailing that went into a historic town house's entrance would be almost unimaginable today. The entrance was a statement of wealth and taste. For the modern owner, however, preserving workmanship and detailing of a front entrance can be a huge expense and involve a dizzying array of artisans, from woodworkers to stone sculptors to custom window makers.

HISTORY

The fashion of the day dictated the style of town house front entrances. Federal doorways had semielliptical fanlight windows over the door and delicate friezes with classical motifs. Greek Revival entries had Doric columns, while later Italianate ones were known for their soaring hand-carved double doors. Until the Greek Revival, front doors were solid, consisting of panes of wood held together by a frame. As glass became cheaper and stronger, larger panes were incorporated into double entrance doors that were as tall as nine feet. Clear at first, the glass itself became increasingly decorative, with etching, stained glass, and glazing.

ON STOOPS

Dutch settlers brought the concept of a stoop to North American town houses. The word comes from the Dutch *stoep,* meaning "small porch." In the Netherlands, the stoop's role was to elevate the main floor of a house above-ground to protect it from flooding. The North American stoop—a low flight of steps built of a material such as brownstone, marble, or iron—has functioned as an ornamental feature. In a single-family residence, the stoop gave formal access to the parlor floor, while the street entrance, usually a few steps below grade, opened onto the garden level.

DOOR MAINTENANCE Today it is almost impossible to buy off-the-shelf replacement doors for a classic town house (even though many of the original were ordered from architectural catalogs), which is a good argument for maintaining the one you've got. A wood door can last for a hundred years or more, or even indefinitely, if it is well preserved. To maintain a front door, the paint or varnish should be redone every five to ten years. The door should be wiped clean periodically and resealed annually with a marine-grade varnish.

RESTORE OR REPLACE? Signs that a door is in poor condition include: failing joinery (where the stiles meet the rails), wood rot, twisting, missing pieces, and deterioration at the door's sill. If your town house door exhibits any of these problems, you'll have to decide between restoring or replacing. Both routes are expensive.

Restoring a door is a painstaking process that involves replacing rotted and missing sections with new matching wood. It can be worth it in order to retain a true antique made of old-growth wood. To replace a door, use an experienced door craftsman. Get recommendations from neighbors and local preservation agencies to find an artisan who can replicate the original and create an almost identical substitute. Though the templates are now done on a computer, a door is still crafted almost entirely by hand.

THE BRAHMIN

Date built: 1835 | Width: 36 feet | Stories: 5 | Square footage: 10,000 | Bedrooms: 5 | Fireplaces: 7
Year purchased: 2001 | Length of renovation: 3 years | House style: Greek Revival

The 1835 Greek Revival town house on Mount Vernon Place could be the setting for a Henry James novel, and in fact, the author used to live around the corner on a street he once declared the most respectable in America. The house, enviable for its corner location, boasts three sunny exposures and five bedrooms, and is thought by some to have been designed by Alexander Parris, one of America's early architects.

The town house would once have been decorated with the most fashionable furniture and fabrics imported from Europe, and a sizable household staff would have attended to the care and upkeep of the residence's almost ten thousand square feet. It's a lifestyle that few today can replicate, and indeed the building has lost many of its decorative flourishes in the years

PREVIOUS SPREAD, LEFT: In the dramatic foyer, the skyblue ceiling reaches to the bottom of the spiral stair, and the walls are covered in hibiscus-print wallpaper.

ABOVE: Artist David Moriarty painted the dining room walls with scenes of Philadelphia, the homeowner's native city. RIGHT AND OPPOSITE: Unlike many formal dining rooms, which are used only for special occasions, this one was designed to be multifunctional, with club chairs and loveseats for relaxing, and a square table that extends to fifteen feet for formal dining.

it served as offices for the Unitarian Church's Beacon Press. When a young family bought the town house in 2001 and hired interior designer Heidi Pribell to oversee the renovation, Pribell knew she had a rare opportunity to bring a classic Boston town house back to its original grandeur.

Pribell, who dealt in antiques before starting her Boston interior design practice, has a rare talent for combining her connoisseur's eye with bravura turns of color and pattern. She had earned the clients' trust several years earlier when the couple asked her to check out a condominium they were considering buying in an old Boston apartment building. She asked to see the basement and there discovered a valuable antique mantelpiece lying in a dusty pile. She recognized its similarity to one brought to Boston in the early nineteenth century by Thomas Appleton, a former American consul to Italy. "The developers were thrilled to make the sale and gave them the mantel," Pribell says. "It turned out to be worth a large sum of money."

The family installed the mantel when they moved to the town house on Mount Vernon Place. It was the first of many treasures that would restore the home to its place as a showpiece for fine furnishings and the decorative arts. Pribell sought out other antiques appropriate to a Boston home of the early nineteenth century. She found a rare pair of English crystal chandeliers (circa 1830) for the front and rear parlors. A set of classical gondola-form chairs from the estate of Fred Hughes, Andy

Warhol's business partner, was purchased for the parlor dining room. Anything that couldn't be found was custom designed, from the lavish tasseled and swagged silk taffeta window treatments throughout the house to the crotched mahogany veneer doors with their ring-turned crystal knobs.

Pribell's fearless eye for color is apparent in the master bedroom suite. In just one room, a Prussian blue and willow green custom carpet is paired with a gold damask wall covering, while a gold medallion centers the green ceiling. There's a nineteenth-century Boston chaise lounge covered in a colorful cut-velvet upholstery fabric, and the windows are draped in gold-, red-, and green-striped silk taffeta. "It's vibrant and playful," Pribell says, "yet all the patterns are steeped in historical references."

The renovation took three years and incorporated every modern amenity, from

OPPOSITE: The mantel, brought with the owners from their last home, was installed in a sunny family dining room located off the garden-level kitchen. LEFT: In the master bedroom, the tiger maple and rosewood bed, specially made for the house by a cabinetmaker in Philadelphia, has a headboard that was designed to conform to the curve of the wall. ABOVE: Upstairs, in the attic, a mahogany door follows the arc of the spiral stair hall.

FOLLOWING SPREAD, LEFT: In a powder room, a Biedermeier plant stand was converted into a sink. The mirror, made in Boston, is an antique dating from the same period as the house. RIGHT: The master bedroom has a nineteenth-century Boston chaise upholstered with Victorian-style button-tufted upholstery. The silk draperies, custom-made in England, are loaded with passementerie details, from rope swags to rosettes.

a media room to a home gym and elevator. Still, much of the original house was saved, including the original interior window shutters and seats, and four Portoro and Bardiglio Cappella marble fireplaces. The few salvageable floorboards were recycled into tabletops and kitchen beams.

The town house's most spectacular feature is also original: a spiral staircase that coils from the foyer to the attic floor (see page 34). If that were not eye-catching enough, the stairwell's walls, which are twenty-five feet high in the foyer, are papered in a lavish hibiscus print by the French firm Boussac. For a final flourish, Pribell covered the foyer floor in black and white cushion-cut marble tile. The lavish finishings are in keeping with the town house's original decor. Henry James would surely have approved.

FORGOTTEN GRANDEUR

|TROY, NEW YORK|

Date built: 1852–54 | Width: 54 feet | Stories: 4 | Square footage: 9,000 | Bedrooms: 7 | Fireplaces: 5
Year purchased: 2001 | Length of renovation: 10 months | House style: Italianate

The restoration of one of the grandest houses in town was a milestone for Troy, once one of the wealthiest communities in the nation. The stately Italianate brownstone, fifty-four feet wide and occupying two full lots, had an illustrious history. Built between 1852 and 1854, it had been the residence of Uri Gilbert, a stagecoach maker and two-time mayor of Troy. It had a magnificent view of the town square and had survived into the twenty-first century with much of its charm intact, from the original gasolier still hanging in the front ballroom to the two-story brick carriage house in the rear courtyard, where the worn green wooden window frames still have grooves from the horses that used to gnaw on them.

RIGHT: The parlor's original console mirror was found half-rotted and sitting in dirt in the carriage house. The piece, which weighs five-hundred pounds, took six months to restore. OPPOSITE: The elaborate front parlor—known in Troy as a ballroom—is furnished in true period style with antiques the current owner bought largely at country auctions. Antiques dealer Zane Z. Studenroth spent months hand-cleaning the room's original 1850s gasolier, which had been covered in so much grime it appeared to be gray and was discovered to have the crystals hanging upside down. He was thrilled to find a perfect match for the fixture's many missing lusters and shade holders at W. N. de Sherbinin Products, a Connecticut lamp parts dealer.

But like so many of the town houses on this once-elegant block, this glorious brownstone was in serious disrepair. A local arts center had owned and used the town house for years as an office and gallery space. With few funds for upkeep and repair, the group discovered that the house was crumbling around them. There were puddles in the basement, the back porch was falling off, and the elegant gasolier was covered in soot. The house went on the market and stayed there for four years. At last, a couple of local preservationists, Lynn Kopka and Joseph P. Abbey, bought the house, largely to save it from the fate of so many of the neighborhood's historic town houses, which real estate developers had purchased and carved into smaller apartments.

In the entrance hall, the floor was so filthy that the parquet's intricate geometric pattern was barely visible. Wood floor experts were brought in to clean and repair the inlay, rebuilding the floor's diamond design with perfectly matching slices of quartersawn wood. Decorative plaster specialists arrived to rebuild missing sections of the dining room's plaster cornice, which was water damaged. On the floor in the carriage house, under several layers of dirt, the new owners made a startling discovery: the ballroom's crowning feature, a hand-carved rosewood console—a spectacular piece with Doric columns, gilding, hand-painted decoration, and a five-hundred-pound mirror. The glass was beyond repair, and the wood half rotted through. The restoration of the antique console would take six months at a cost of $12,000. Eventually the owners became overwhelmed by the scope and expense of preserving their nine-thousand-square-foot historic house. "We were hemorrhaging money," Kopka admits.

OPPOSITE: A valuable Herter Brothers mantel was discovered in the house in two parts: the mirror was in one room, and the mantel in another. During the renovation the sections were recombined and installed in this northeast salon. LEFT: The formal dining room, which had suffered serious water damage, was completely reconstructed by specialized artisans. The red damask wallpaper, from Stroheim & Romann, creates a Victorian effect. ABOVE: This wall between the club room and the library had been removed during a previous renovation. The owners had it re-created, installing an antique marble mantel and wall molding to match the others in the space.

The solution was an unusual real estate switch. They had planned to live in the Gilbert house and had signed a contract with another couple, Warren and Pam Abele, to sell them their former home, a town house just three doors down the street. They asked the couple whether they would consider buying the larger Gilbert house instead. To their surprise, they happily agreed, and the houses were swapped. The new owners were a retired couple with a love of historic houses. Fortunately they had a head start: before she sold the home, Kopka had organized a charity showhouse,

in which local interior designers offered their services to decorate the rooms. Pam Abele, who furnished the house, purchased the elaborate curtain treatments that had been confected for the showhouse and started frequenting local auctions to find antiques to furnish the vast house.

When Gilbert lived here, the house had four full-time servants, including a seamstress and coachman, to keep everything moving smoothly. The Abeles, whose young granddaughters live down the street with their parents, don't live that way and do much of the upkeep themselves. "You never get done with a house like this," Pam Abele admits. "But you have to live someplace: why not in a lovely house?"

OPPOSITE: In the master bedroom, the carved four-poster bed is a family heirloom. ABOVE: A guest bedroom has antique adult and child-size beds and shimmering chinoiserie wallpaper.

BROWNSTONE

Brownstone, the chocolate brown veneer that was all the rage in the nineteenth century along the eastern seaboard, has a majestic elegance. However, the real thing is rarely used any longer because of its fragility. Most brownstone facades today consist of tinted stucco veneers. Repairing or replacing brownstone is labor intensive and a major investment for any homeowner.

HISTORY

Brownstone is a sedimentary stone made up of grains of sand and other minerals held together by natural cementing agents such as ferric oxide (rust), which gives the material its dark brown or reddish brown color. The stone deposits are two hundred million years old, dating back to when continental drift created basins filled with sand and mud. This sediment—composed of quartz, mica, and feldspar—became brownstone.

In 1650, an English tomb carver found a wedge of the chocolate brown sandstone on the banks of the Connecticut River. The material would come to define much of the New York cityscape. It was quarried in several locations, including Massachusetts, New Jersey, and Pennsylvania, but the most active source was in Portland, Connecticut, where it could easily be ferried across the Northeast via the Connecticut River.

Brownstone really took off in the nineteenth century, during the years the essayist Lewis Mumford later called "the Brown Decades"—when Romantic-minded artists and intellectuals craved a return to nature. Brownstone was suitably earthy and far less expensive than such classical materials as granite, limestone, and marble. By 1880, New York City's federal census reports that 78.6 percent of the city's buildings made of stone were all or part brownstone. The soft material could be applied over a brick facade or carved into decorative flourishes, from bas-reliefs to architraves.

A HABIT OF PEELING Brownstone is highly porous and prone to water damage and a condition known as spalling, or flaking, which is caused when moisture gets between its sedimentary layers and then freezes and expands. This is particularly true when the material is improperly applied, as it frequently was in the nineteenth century. The sandstone needs to be dried for up to six months after being quarried, and applied the same way it lies in the earth, with its end-grain running left to right. A brownstone surface is four to six inches thick. The material became so notorious for flaking that by 1900 it was out of style, and by the 1930s, the last brownstone quarries were closed.

GOOD SUBSTITUTES We've come a long way since the misguided brownstone fixes of earlier generations, which ranged from applying layers of paint to encasing the stone in aluminum siding or faux brick. An alternative method, based on ancient Mediterranean stucco techniques brought to North America by European craftsmen, has evolved into a more durable substitute. "It in itself is an art form," says Alex Herrera, director of technical services for the New York Landmarks Conservancy. "It's all handmade and hand-carved. The artisans can do acanthus scrolls, capitals, leaves, and flowers. It takes craftsmanship."

CARING FOR AND REPAIRING

Brownstone repair is not a do-it-yourself project. Ask your local architectural preservation agency for expert referrals. Depending on the extent of the damage, a brownstone facade will either need patching or complete refacing. In both cases, the weathered surface of the stone is chipped back with hammers and chisels until a rough, pockmarked surface remains. Three layers of stucco are then applied by hand: the first layer is applied to the rough undersurface, in a technique known as "keying in." The second layer is used to build up the contours of the surface, and the final layer consists of stucco with pigment for color. Getting the stucco to match existing brownstone is tricky, which is why most masons will advise against patches unless the damage is minor. ("It usually isn't," Herrera warns.) A full brownstone facade stucco replacement can cost upward of $50,000 and will take ten to twelve weeks.

THE RETURN OF BROWNSTONE

In the 1990s, a geologist named Mike Meehan leased part of the historic Portland quarry and began quarrying true brownstone for the first time in sixty years. His company, Portland Brownstone Quarries, has since provided the genuine article for restoration work from Maine to South Carolina. Though they have supplied brownstone for town houses, most of their customers are larger institutions, owing to the high cost of the material—a full facade replacement, including removal of the old stone, runs about $150 a square foot just for the flat surface. For a twenty-foot-wide, five-story brownstone, the tab for a true Portland brownstone facade would be a minimum of $150,000.

Old Meets New

HOW DO YOU GIVE an old house new life, without destroying its original charm? The homeowners in this section are a diverse lot: they include a movie star, a fashion designer, a Southern belle, and a pair of eccentric set designers from Baltimore. What links them is a shared passion for restoration and a belief in the inherent flexibility of the classic town house model.

A young mother from France, her heart set on moving into a modernist loft, surprises herself by falling for the timeless proportions of an 1830s Brooklyn row house. In Montreal, an architect ponders how to expand her historic Tudor Gothic town house without resorting to artifice or architectural incongruity. And in Greenwich Village, the actress Julianne Moore, having searched for years for the quintessential classic town house, finally finds it and hires a cutting-edge design firm to both restore it to perfection and make it modern.

True, there are stairs to climb and mantels to dust. But there are also stoops to sit on, high-ceilinged rooms with tall windows, and formal parlors filled with the ornament and craft of an earlier time. And there are clever adaptations: rooms that once housed live-in servants are converted into home offices or media dens, and bedrooms (in homes that sometimes predate plumbing) are transformed into showpiece bathrooms. Dark, narrow interiors are freshened with lighting, color, and other architectural tricks. Just as these historic town houses have been adapted for the present, their owners have learned to savor the pleasures of the past.

STAR TURN

Date built: 1839 | Width: 21 feet | Stories: 5 | Square footage: 5,000 | Bedrooms: 4 | Fireplaces: 7
Year purchased: 2003 | Length of renovation: 18 months | House style: Greek Revival

"I don't like Federal," the actress Julianne Moore declares. "The proportions make my head hurt." She is seated at her desk, in the front parlor of her Greek Revival town house, and she is just getting started. "I don't like Victorian," she says. "It's too ornate. I do like Italianate, but those homes are ridiculously expensive. Then even when I do find a house I like, with nice proportions, too often it's had the soul renovated out of it."

Moore is a movie star who has lit up the screen in films such as *The End of the Affair* and *Far from Heaven*. She is also an architecture and design buff and a connoisseur in particular of New York City town houses. After all, she had searched for over a decade for the perfect brownstone, and at one point even moved her family—husband and

film director Bart Freundlich, and their two children, Caleb and Liv—into a loft in downtown Manhattan. But she never entirely gave up her search for a town house, and then she found it. The 1839 house in Greenwich Village, built by a merchant, had water damage and had been carved up into apartments. However, many elements from the original house had survived, such as the staircase and the traditional floorboards and hallways. Moore had always loved Greek Revival row houses for their tall, airy rooms and elegant details, and she was immediately smitten.

Her goal was to return the house to its original design as a single-family home while adding such modern amenities as an eat-in kitchen, central air-conditioning, and bathrooms on every floor. She enlisted her husband's brother, architect Oliver Freundlich, and his partners at Brooklyn-based MADE architecture firm, to oversee the renovation. Not wanting to disturb the dimensions of the front and back rooms, the architects devised a clever solution: a shaft runs down the center of the building housing such modern mechanics as plumbing, electricity, and air handlers to pump central air-conditioning onto each floor. Everything that could be saved, from the plasterwork to the pine-plank floorboards, was placed in storage while the house was reengineered.

PREVIOUS SPREAD, LEFT: The home's original pine floors were dyed with potassium dichromate in an antique process used to darken wood. RIGHT: Julianne Moore, who decorated her own house, chose an earthy palette of grays and browns to offset her collection of midcentury furnishings. The living room's decor includes a George Nakashima coffee table and an Eames rocking chair. "I think dark colors make a strong statement, in a town house," Moore says. OPPOSITE: Moore turned the front parlor into her home office, furnishing it with an Isamu Noguchi lantern, a pair of French chairs, and a pony-skin rug. "I didn't want the parlor to become the fancy room that no one ever uses," she says. THIS PAGE: The home mixes period details, such as this original shutter (right) and a Doric column in a Greek Revival doorway (far right) with modern design—like this twentieth-century Italian sconce (below).

Sculpture House, a New York firm specializing in plasterwork since the early 1900s, re-created moldings wherever they were missing. They look visibly new next to the older, original ones with their edges softened by layers of paint and decades of wear. Freundlich says the contrast is deliberate, part of an attempt to be respectful of the building without trying to fake authenticity. In fact, Moore was determined that the quirkiness of the house come through intact. The floors still squeak and the house leans about a half-inch to one side. "I love the fact that the house is crooked," she says. "It drove the workers crazy. They kept wanting to level it out. But I said no, that is part of the house."

The actress does all her own decorating. Her counterintuitive color scheme features such dark earth tones as brown, gray, and black, paired with off-white. "Some people would paint a dark town house all white or brighten it up, but I don't like a lot of color," she says. The palette not only looks dramatic but also helps create a bridge between the historic proportions of the house and the modernist furniture Moore collects. "One of my favorite juxtapositions is modern furniture in a really old house," she says. "You see that a lot in Europe."

Moore and the architects thought carefully about the vertical lifestyle implicit in row house living. In order to minimize trips up and down stairs, she requested a large coat closet by the ground-floor entrance, two laundry rooms—one downstairs and another upstairs—and a bathroom on every level. The playroom was placed near the upstairs bedrooms so that she wouldn't be constantly picking up toys scattered throughout the house. Another indulgence was a central vacuuming system.

With two young children to tend to, she is up and down her home's four stories, floorboards creaking as she goes. After years of dreaming about her perfect town house, she wouldn't have it any other way.

ABOVE: The kitchen is located on the home's ground level, off the garden, where it would have been in the nineteenth century. The room retains its original hearth and beamed ceiling. To accommodate a modern open-plan kitchen and dining area, the space was enlarged by extending it into the hallway. A nineteen-foot-wide entryway is supported by steel beams. The kitchen island has Boffi cabinetry, a Carrara-marble worktop, and vintage barstools. OPPOSITE: New French doors separate the dining area from the garden.

FOLLOWING SPREAD, LEFT: "How do you fit a movie-star bathroom into a town house floor?" asks Moore's architect, her brother-in-law Oliver Freundlich of MADE architecture. The answer was to turn an entire bedroom into a luxurious bath. The focal point is a bathtub with a marble surround that matches the room's classical mantel.

RESTORATION NOTES ORNAMENTAL PLASTER

Ornamental plasterwork is highly durable and "should last forever," says Michael Perrotta, manager of Sculpture House, the New York City plaster firm that worked on Julianne Moore and Bart Freundlich's restoration. "What usually happens is that, over the years, people paint over it. When there are fifteen to twenty layers of paint, which is typical in an old town house, you don't see the detail anymore." Decorative moldings can also fall prey to water damage, structural movement in a house, or the vagaries of taste.

HISTORY

Egg and dart, bead and barrel, acanthus-leaf and lamb's-tongue: the vocabulary of ornamental plaster is as exotic to the modern eye as the decorative flourish these ornamental plaster patterns add to a room. Any town house built from the mid-eighteenth century until the 1930s would have had decorative plasterwork, from the cornices to coffered ceilings to ceiling medallions—the bigger the budget, the more elaborate the ornamentation. The visual vocabulary was inspired by the architecture of ancient Greece and Rome, with their five classical orders: Doric, Ionic, Corinthian, Tuscan, and Composite. The ancient Greeks used ornament to create visual interest with highlights and shadows. Plaster moldings—so called because they were cast in molds—would change according to architectural fashions, from the delicate Adamesque styles of the Federal period to the floral friezes of the Victorian town house. Until the late nineteenth century most plaster in America was made of crushed limestone or shell deposits and often mixed with cattle hair. Gypsum plaster (also known as Plaster of Paris), a soft mineral composed of calcium sulfate, was later preferred because it dries quickly and has a harder finish.

ARTISANAL PLASTER Traditional-style ornamental plaster is still made by artisans skilled in the old techniques. There are two types: "run in place" plaster, which is produced on-site; and plaster that is cast in molds in a workshop. Ornaments such as ceiling medallions, brackets, and dentils are usually cast in molds off-site.

At the Moore/Freundlich house, sections of rosettes were missing from the cornice. Sculpture House took a section of the existing decoration and removed multiple layers of paint to restore it to its original condition. This was used to create a rubber mold of the decoration, which was then used to create new plaster castings to match the originals. These were brought back to the house and attached to the wall with screws and adhesives. In certain cases (if a ceiling rosette is difficult to take down, for instance), plaster artisans will need to create ornamental plaster on-site, a challenging process that involves two workers, one

to mix the plaster and the other to take a template of the ornament and "run" the new pieces up to the ceiling.

OFF THE SHELF Ornamental plasterwork is painstakingly made by hand, with prices to match. If the budget doesn't permit the real thing, there are less expensive alternatives. Founded in 1883, Chicago's Decorators Supply (see Where to Find It, page 270) has hundreds of original molds for ornamental plaster and wood ornaments, from cameo-and-rosette ceiling medallions to crown-acanthus and run-coin crown molding. The company's vice president, Jack Meingast, says homeowners can send the firm a picture of their existing moldings. "Sixty percent of the time we still have it," Meingast says. If they don't, you can send them a three-foot section, and they will reproduce an exact copy. Polyurethane and resin moldings, which are light and easy to install, are increasing in popularity.

THE NOSTALGIC

|BROOKLYN HEIGHTS, BROOKLYN|

Date built: Circa 1865 | Width: 25 feet | Stories: 5 | Square footage: 5,250 | Bedrooms: 7 | Fireplaces: 8
Year purchased: Middle two floors in 1986; bottom two floors in 2001: top floor in 2004 | Length of renovation:
2 years for the first renovation; 1 year for the second | House style: Italianate

The Italianate brownstone, circa 1865, is unusually
well preserved, from the antique brass door buzzer to the
plasterwork inside on the parlor floor, where acanthus-leaf
corbeils and rosettes decorate the perimeter of the ceilings. The owner, Kathryn Scott,
in a floor-length, pearl gray silk dress, has the genteel good manners of an earlier era as
she walks through her home, pointing out details like the engraved switch plates in every
room. The enormous kitchen has the ambience of a turn-of-the-century library, with glass-
fronted wooden cabinets stretching floor to ceiling, the china and sterling silver at the top
reached with the help of a wooden library ladder.

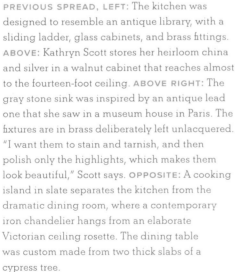

PREVIOUS SPREAD, LEFT: The kitchen was designed to resemble an antique library, with a sliding ladder, glass cabinets, and brass fittings. ABOVE: Kathryn Scott stores her heirloom china and silver in a walnut cabinet that reaches almost to the fourteen-foot ceiling. ABOVE RIGHT: The gray stone sink was inspired by an antique lead one that she saw in a museum house in Paris. The fixtures are in brass deliberately left unlacquered. "I want them to stain and tarnish, and then polish only the highlights, which makes them look beautiful," Scott says. OPPOSITE: A cooking island in slate separates the kitchen from the dramatic dining room, where a contemporary iron chandelier hangs from an elaborate Victorian ceiling rosette. The dining table was custom made from two thick slabs of a cypress tree.

In fact, it is all an artful illusion. An artist and self-taught interior designer from Houston, Texas, Scott moved to New York in the 1980s and apprenticed to New York design icons Leila and Massimo Vignelli. She admired the Vignellis' crisp minimalism and eventually became their employee. But she had grown up with antiques and couldn't imagine a life as a pure modernist. She was drawn to a romantic idea of the past and decided to conjure the vanished universe of her imagination through design and craft.

As she walked the streets of New York, the elegant Sutton Place town house of the movie *Auntie Mame* in her head, she decided that living in a historic town house would be an essential component of the fantasy. She was twenty-eight when she moved in the 1980s into her brownstone in Brooklyn Heights, one of New York's oldest neighborhoods. The house had potential, but it was not yet the elegant brownstone Scott expected it to be. The building had belonged for many years to the minister of nearby Saint Ann's Church, a Gothic gem still visible from Scott's rear windows. The former owner had removed the front stoop and the Italianate facade decorations and turned the upper floors into a boardinghouse. Inside, the plaster ceilings were hidden by dropped ceilings.

When she found it, the five-story brownstone was being converted into a cooperatively owned apartment building. Scott purchased one of the three units—an apartment comprising the third and fourth floors. It was an extravagant purchase for a young single woman—or so her relatives thought. They told her she was making a foolish investment and, indeed, she struggled for several years just to keep the two floors. Owning an entire town house would have seemed impossible. But when her mother moved in with Scott in 2002, she purchased the parlor and bottom floor, which were for sale. Two years later, the owner of the top floor decided to sell, and she bought it to use as a rental apartment.

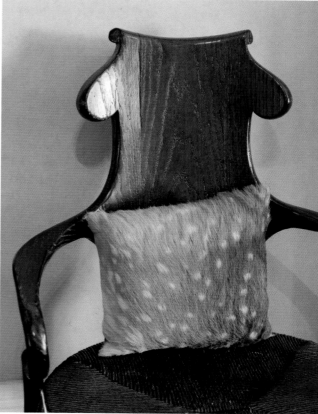

OPPOSITE: The living room's Rossa Verona antique marble mantel was the inspiration for the room's golden palette of oranges and reds. The walls were plastered in oatmeal-hued fresco, while the chimney mantel was decorated in terracotta–tinted encaustic, a technique in which pigments are added to hot wax. Artisans were brought in to repair the ceiling's crown molding and reproduce missing corbeils and sections of ball trim. The furnishings include several pieces Scott designed and custom-made in Shanghai, where her artist-husband, Wenda Gu, was born. ABOVE: Scott sketched a template for a new staircase railing and had it cut with a laserjet out of steel panels. TOP RIGHT: The chair is by Rose Tarlow Melrose House. BOTTOM RIGHT: The red blocks are Wenda Gu's hand-carved stone chops, which he uses to stamp his ink paintings.

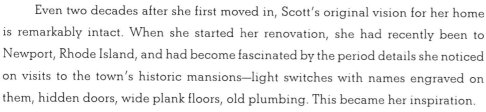

Even two decades after she first moved in, Scott's original vision for her home is remarkably intact. When she started her renovation, she had recently been to Newport, Rhode Island, and had become fascinated by the period details she noticed on visits to the town's historic mansions—light switches with names engraved on them, hidden doors, wide plank floors, old plumbing. This became her inspiration.

Scott used her renovation as a university of sorts on updating and decorating a town house. She became both her own designer and client and even worked on the site every day as a construction worker. She assisted the carpenter, hammered pegs, helped make French doors, and sanded moldings. She made a steel template for the staircase, sketching the design on-site, selected lumber for the floors, and researched vintage plumbing fixtures.

Since many of the brownstone's original details had been removed, she set out to put them back. This involved a great deal of detective work. She visited the brownstone next door, a mirror image of her own, to study the plasterwork and copied the two-inch-thick base molding in the neighbor's parlor for her own living room. A plaster artisan reproduced any moldings that were missing around door archways

Scott painted her bedroom orange—a shade inspired by terra-cotta—soon after moving into the town house. The paint was applied with a decorative technique known as strié, which gives the appearance of a silk wall covering. The antique Sheraton field bed belonged to her grandmother. Beside it sits her grandfather's World War II navy trunk, which her grandmother decorated with painted flowers after the war. The nightstands are Qing Dynasty antiques from Shanghai.

TOP LEFT: Scott's daughter, Simone (above), has a reproduction Ming Dynasty Chinese bed in her room. TOP RIGHT: The old-fashioned linen closet has sliding drawers in curly maple with brass plates. OPPOSITE: Scott searched at auctions and contacted salvage dealers to find vintage plumbing fixtures, like this porcelain footed bathtub in the master bathroom from Urban Archaeology.
FOLLOWING SPREAD, LEFT: In a guest bedroom, an antique Biedermeier bed purchased on eBay has a handmade mattress. RIGHT: A cherry tree blooms inthe rear garden, which is nestled between neighboring houses.

in her home. For her bathrooms, she sought out vintage bathtubs, sinks, and antique plumbing fixtures. The walls, inspired by Italian palazzos, were painted in a strié finish, a technique that resembles silk wall coverings.

When she absorbed the brownstone's lower two floors, Scott created an apartment for her mother on the bottom, or garden, level. By that point, she needed more space, as she now had a family: her husband is Wenda Gu, an acclaimed artist from China, and they have a young child, Simone. Now a successful interior designer with offices in New York and Shanghai, Scott took advantage of her newly acquired parlor floor to showcase her talents. This time she had the budget for real plaster walls in the living room; she also restored the ornate plaster details on the ceilings, simplifying the design by using central medallions and cornices of intricately carved plaster trim. The kitchen is especially grand, with its walnut counters, slate-topped island, and glass-and-verdigree pendants from the British lighting maker Charles Edwards.

In a house that seems otherwise authentic to its period, the kitchen is anachronistic with its modern appliances and open placement next to the dining room. The original kitchen would have been a servants' galley on the garden floor. No matter: the effect is to transport its occupants into an earlier time, one when the smallest details—down to the cremone bolts on the windows—mattered and when utilitarian objects were made by hand to last a lifetime.

STRAIGHT AND NARROW

|HISTORIC DISTRICT, SAVANNAH|

Date built: 1854 | Width: 15 feet | Stories: 3 | Square footage: 1,500 | Bedrooms: 2 | Fireplaces: 5
Year purchased: 1999 | Length of renovation: 18 months | House style: Greek Revival

Jeannie Sims is the kind of outsize personality that Savannah seems to draw like butterflies to milkweed—bright red lipstick, large sunglasses, animal prints, and a penchant for grand gestures that extends to her decor. "I love the bling," she says, showing off her collections of mercury glass and antique English silver. That she lives in one of the smallest row houses in town comes as a surprise, but not when you learn how she made the most of it.

In the nineteenth century, a standard property lot in Savannah was sixty feet wide. Developers created rows of two or even three town houses on these lots. But only one builder had the ingenuity—some would say audacity—to create a row of four houses, each just fifteen feet wide, on a single block facing Chatham Square. Sims's house is the third

from the left. Christian Sottile, a Savannah-based urban planner and college professor, considers the houses unusual in a town of remarkable architecture. He says this developer, trying to make the most of his real estate, "skinned the cat in a new way." Since there wasn't enough room facing the street for four staircases and entries, he cleverly placed two of the stoops on the outside edges of the end units.

Sims says she was drawn to the brick-and-stucco house both for its view of the square—a serene spot with live oak trees and park benches—and the home's modest cost. It had architectural assets such as original fireplaces and antique plank floors. The facade was built of Savannah gray brick, a unique building material now coveted by collectors. But there were serious deficits. The porch, windows, and stairs all needed replacing. The exposed-brick walls were so thin that Sims could see through the mortar into her neighbor's living room. Most important, at fifteen feet wide and thirty-seven feet deep, the town house was simply too small for Sims's extensive wish list of amenities: "I wanted a slick kitchen, a powder room downstairs, a porch on the parlor floor, a second bedroom, and a bathroom upstairs," she says.

She hired Savannah architect Daniel E. Snyder to reconfigure the house. To create more livable space, he designed a three-story addition that extends into the garden at the rear of the house. Savannah's strict zoning rules forbid building on more than 75 percent of a lot line—and with Snyder a member of the Savannah Historic District Board of Review, he was bound to go strictly by the book. He carefully measured out every legal and available inch.

Fortunately for Sims, her Savannah gray bricks were in excellent condition. However, most everything else needed replacing. Snyder added black shutters to the facade to frame the new nine-over-nine paned windows. The two fireplaces were relined and converted to gas, their plain wood mantels gussied up with architectural appliqués. The threadbare brick walls inside the house were insulated and covered in drywall.

Both Sims and her architect fell in love with the old floors, which were made of heart pine, the same wood flooring used in Thomas Jefferson's Monticello and George Washington's Mount Vernon. The wood, rare today, was cut from southern

longleaf pines mature enough to have developed heartwood, a process that can take up to five hundred years. Strong and durable, it was a favorite building material of the early American colonists, who used heart pine for everything from shipbuilding to log cabins. But while the trees once covered 41 percent of the landmass in the Deep South, today fewer than ten thousand acres remain, all in protected forests. The architect says that he was repeatedly warned by floor refinishers that the wood in Sims's house was beyond repair. He convinced her that with special care, the floorboards could be salvaged. He found an expert refinisher who took care not to oversand the planks and who finished them with a high-gloss lacquer. "Because of their age and width, they have that combination of crudeness and hyperelegance," Snyder says. "They were the greatest gift to the house."

OPPOSITE: In the living room French doors lead out to the new porch. The room has an antique Irish bench covered in a leopard print, a collection of mercury glass, and silver vases by Jonathan Adler. RIGHT: At the other end of the living room blue-gray walls set off the exuberant decor. "High drama, honey, high drama," Sims says. ABOVE: On the top floor, the Chippendale-style railing and high-gloss floors lead to the owner's bedroom.

Sims had inherited many antiques from her parents, who had lived in a Williamsburg-style home in rural Albany, Georgia, including a Chippendale sideboard, an English silver service, and a Regency wardrobe. They were the perfect scale for the house—not too big or too small. Her parents' collection of Chinese export porcelain shares tabletop space with pottery by the hip contemporary designer Jonathan Adler. And her mother's epergne—a silver table centerpiece that is a traditional southern mainstay—overflows with seashells and coral, rather than the usual fruit or flowers.

When Sims hosts one of her frequent parties, the action overflows from the parlor onto the new porch, an outdoor space that functions as an extension of the living room. There is no other place in Savannah quite like it, with its tangle of tropical plants, a painted mural, and a crystal chandelier that on closer inspection turns out to be plastic.

The fifteen-foot-wide house is third from the left in a row of four houses facing Savannah's Chatham Square. To save space, the builder placed two of the four stoops on the outside edges of the end units. The facade was built of Savannah gray brick, a building material now highly sought after by collectors.

WOOD FLOORS

Few features give an old town house more character than antique wood floors, whether they are simple pine planks or elaborately detailed Victorian parquet. For something that takes such a beating, wood—particularly the lumber from centuries-old trees that was used in town house construction prior to the twentieth century—is remarkably long lasting. Any imperfections, such as gaps between planks or squeaky floorboards, seem only to add to a wood floor's charm.

HISTORY

Naturally finished antique wood floors have become an essential component of modern town house decor. But in many cases that is not how they would have originally appeared. Before the nineteenth century, most town house floors were soft wood and meant to be painted. Others—like those made of eastern white pine, popular in the North, and heart pine, used in the South—were left unfinished and maintained by regular mopping with water and lye. Many simple wood floors were never even designed to be exposed. They were subfloors for coverings such as wall-to-wall carpeting, which came into fashion in American homes following the invention of the power loom in 1839. It was only during the Victorian period, when Oriental area rugs came into fashion, that wood floors became finished and more elaborate, with intricate parquetry framing the carpets along the room's borders.

SQUEAKY FLOORS If your floor sags or is creaky, the first thing to do is determine whether it is structurally sound. *Old-House Journal*'s founder Clem Labine suggests these tests to see if your floor has structural issues: (1) Roll a marble or ball across the floor to identify the direction and severity of the sag. (2) Jump up and down. If the floor vibrates and the windows rattle, there is a problem. (3) Walk around the floor to locate loose and springy boards. Obviously, you will want to bring in an expert—a house inspector or an engineer—to check serious structural issues. The fixes can range from minor repairs, such as reinforcing the joists that support the floor, to major work, such as shoring up girders.

GAPS BETWEEN FLOORS As a wood floor ages, its planks expand and contract, and gaps inevitably appear between them. Before attempting repairs, remember that the wood will swell in summer, often remedying the problem. In winter, a humidifier may help to close the gaps. If the spaces are too big even at the height of summer, consider filling them with a flexible paste, filler, or elastic caulk that can adapt to the movement of the wood. For the biggest cracks, narrow wood strips can be added between the boards, but this must be carefully done, as they can often make the problem worse.

BAD BOARDS Replace floorboards with wood that is as close as possible to the original. Wood salvage suppliers near your home might have a match. Ask for wood of the same species, age, and size, with similar ring patterns and cuts (flat cut versus quartersawn, for example). Many homeowners salvage planks from other places in their home, such as the floor of a closet or the attic, and send the wood to a workshop to be remilled. The resawn wood will have the character of old wood, with the advantage of uniformity of width and thickness. The process works best with such woods as oak, chestnut, and northern hard

pine, and costs upward of $8 per linear foot, depending on how much work is involved to remove old nails and prepare the lumber for milling (see Where to Find It, page 270).

HOLES No one expects an antique floor to look pristine; indeed, imperfections lend character to old wood boards. That said, there are ways to fill in the gaps. Small holes, nicks, and scratches can be camouflaged using a touch-up stick made of colored wax. Fill in the hole or scratch, scrape away the excess with a putty knife, and buff. For larger holes, one solution is to install wood grain plugs in the same material. Line up the grain so it matches the surrounding floorboard. Other techniques include filling the hole with wood putty or a mixture of sawdust and white glue, which is then stained to match the floor. Or as Anne Attal (see Simply French, page 133) cleverly devised, a zinc plate with a nail border makes a charming patch (see above).

REVIVE OR REMOVE? Sometimes all you need to revive an old floor finish is a good cleaning with mineral spirits or turpentine; rub gently with fine steel wool to remove old dirt and wax. If the old finish is in bad shape, it will need to be removed. This can be accomplished with paint removers or hand scraping, but usually with power sanding, which works for most kinds of wood floors. But be careful: wood floors can be sanded only a handful of times before they become too thin and must be replaced.

CHOOSING THE FINISH

A finish is a topcoat that protects the floor and adds luster, and sometimes color. There are two types: surface finishes and penetrating finishes. *Surface finishes* create a barrier layer on top of the wood. They include oil- and water-based polyurethanes, shellac, varnish, or paint. They are durable, dry quickly, and are easy to maintain with a light mopping, but the finish can wear away or scratch. *Penetrating finishes* are absorbed into the

wood and then waxed. Such finishes include penetrating sealers and oils such as linseed, made from flaxseeds, and tung, a furniture-grade oil pressed from the nuts of the Chinese tung tree. Both of these organic products have a low sheen, which makes for a very natural look. They are easy to touch up—just recoat the damaged sections. The disadvantage is that penetrating finishes take several days to dry. They also require more maintenance, including a once-a-year application of wax.

COLOR AND SHEEN You'll need to decide whether or not to stain the wood or leave it natural. You'll also have to choose between a high-gloss, low-gloss, or satin (matte) effect. High gloss was the finish of choice for over 150 years, but it can be slippery and scratches easily. Attal chose what she calls a "raw wood" effect, which is popular in Europe: the wood gets stripped and left unfinished and then receives weekly moppings with water and bleach.

DIPLOMATIC CORE

|DUPONT CIRCLE, WASHINGTON, D.C.|

Date built: 1920 | Width: 25 feet | Stories: 5 | Square footage: 9,500 | Bedrooms: 5 | Fireplaces: 5
Year purchased: 1999 | Length of renovation: 2 years | House style: Beaux-Arts

When Darryl Carter was searching for a town house in Washington, D.C., he set his sights on one of the capital's oldest and grandest boulevards, Massachusetts Avenue. Once known as Millionaires' Row, the street is lined with opulent and architecturally diverse adjoined mansions built by such early-twentieth-century tycoons as Edward H. Everett, the Cleveland "bottle cap king," who commissioned a former architect to the sultan of Turkey to build an ornate town house.

Few of these Gilded Age houses would have survived the Great Depression were it not for the foreign governments who bought them and converted them into embassies, many of which remain to this day. But real estate trends have a way of cycling. As wealth has

reentered the capital, Massachusetts Avenue has once again become a coveted residential address. In 1999, Carter, a lawyer turned interior designer, entered a bidding war to purchase a town house from the government of Oman, which had been using it as its chancellery. For Carter, the 1920s Beaux-Arts town house provided a rare sense of privacy in the middle of the city. The back of the house faces Rock Creek Park, a federal park that bisects the nation's capital. From his rear windows, Carter's views take in this leafy oasis along with city views of Georgetown and Dumbarton Oaks. "It's like being in a tree house," Carter says.

At twenty-five feet wide and over nine thousand square feet, the town house had room to spare and an uncommon limestone facade. Indeed, the home's only disappointing feature was its lack of original detail and pedigree. The old floorboards and most of the mantels were gone, as were records on the building and its architect. Still, there were just enough antique features to make the space unique, from a serpentine staircase railing to a Napoleon-style black marble mantel in the living room.

In the home design world, Carter is a rising star. His style—dressy without being too stuffy—has made him a favorite of the shelter magazines. He is increasingly being tapped to design furnishings, such as his lighting collection for the Charleston-based

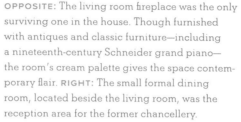

OPPOSITE: The living room fireplace was the only surviving one in the house. Though furnished with antiques and classic furniture—including a nineteenth-century Schneider grand piano—the room's cream palette gives the space contemporary flair. RIGHT: The small formal dining room, located beside the living room, was the reception area for the former chancellery.

lighting firm Urban Electric Company. It made sense to turn the town house into a laboratory for his ideas and a showcase for his elegant but liveable approach.

Carter, who calls himself an architect manqué, began by reenvisioning the layout of the house. His first objective was how to bring in light—a challenge in many town houses, particularly in one that is tall, narrow, and a hundred feet deep. He began by removing walls, creating fewer impediments to the light that entered the home's rectangular layout through its front and back windows. The interior doorways were heightened by three feet and glass transoms added, and milled doors were replaced by ones with paned glass.

There are two kinds of rooms in the house. The formal spaces, like the dining room with its Victorian glass chandelier and polished wood table, are picture-perfect but not always in use. Equally photogenic are the rooms where Carter actually spends most of his time. A highly sociable bachelor, he entertains in the spacious country-style kitchen he created on the parlor floor, where guests gather around a farm table located in an adjoining sunroom. The kitchen itself has white-stained oak cabinetry with wire mesh fronts, honed granite countertops, and a full complement of stainless-steel appliances.

Carter's study was designed to resemble a classic Washington library, with tufted-leather sofas and wainscoted walls. "But I tried to be irreverent," Carter says, "and painted them white." In fact, his sense of humor and panache are everywhere in the decor: in a reading room on the top floor of the town house, where his two large

OPPOSITE: The country-style kitchen (visible from the second-floor landing, above) has a set of French doors leading to a sunny breakfast room, which in turn leads to a terrace with a view of Washington's Rock Creek Park.

FOLLOWING SPREAD, LEFT: The master bedroom suite is designed to serve as independent quarters, consisting of a bedroom, a den, and an expansive bathroom and home gym. RIGHT: According to the dealer, the matching vintage bathtubs were reclaimed from the nearby Russian embassy.

and feisty dogs have free rein, you have to look twice to notice that the animals' favorite perch, a wing chair, is not actually leather but its more practical cousin—vinyl.

Another well-used space is a master bedroom suite that occupies the entire third floor of the town house. Carter says he designed it to function like a self-contained apartment. In addition to the vast bedroom with a four-poster bed, there is a separate room for reading and watching television, and a home gym with a view of the park. Perhaps the town house's slyest touch is in the master bathroom, where Carter installed a pair of vintage bathtubs that reportedly came out of the former Russian embassy, one of his neighbors. The effect is pure spectacle, fittingly since Carter admits he is "more of a shower person." It goes without saying that here on Millionaires' Row, there is a separate shower room, too.

SOUL SURVIVOR

|FORT GREENE, BROOKLYN|

Date built: 1860 | Width: 20 feet | Stories: 4 | Square footage: 3,600 | Bedrooms: 5 | Fireplaces: 7
Year purchased: 2005 | Length of renovation: 12 months | House style: Italianate

Built in 1860, the Italianate brownstone in Brooklyn's Fort Greene neighborhood was showing its age. Yet there were signs everywhere—from the lavish draperies to the elaborate framed mirrors—that it had once been cherished. Meanwhile, the sales contract came with an unusual stipulation: the buyer of the house would be required to erect a commemorative plaque outside in honor of the previous owner, Larry Caparaso, a neighborhood fixture known as Mr. Larry, who had lived on the brownstone-lined street, South Elliott Place, for decades. The buyers, Peter Edge and Mariano Puente, found the stipulation moving. "Larry loved his house and you could tell," Puente says. "And that's what was so appealing to us: that we could help save a historic property." Edge, who was born in England,

OPPOSITE: The rear parlor has a loftlike scale that is accentuated by the low-lying lines of a modern sectional sofa and leather-topped 1950s tables. A floor-to-ceiling mirror in a curved black frame acts as a "third window," says Mariano Puente, reflecting light into the dark space. ABOVE: The mantel in the dining room, located on the first floor off the kitchen, was black with grime. After a cleaning, the Carrara stone was pure white, coordinating with the marble top of Eero Saarinen's dining table.

is a music producer who has discovered and developed such soul artists as Alicia Keys, Dido, and Angie Stone. Puente is an Argentina native who designs modish interiors for a fashionable crowd through his Manhattan-based firm Mariano Design. They are devout Buddhists who met at an ashram and maintain a meditation room in their home. To them, the goal of their renovation was to restore what they call the "chi" of their house, referring to the Chinese word for the natural energy of the universe. They love modern furnishings and wanted a house equipped with the latest technology, from built-in music speakers to central air-conditioning. But their first priority was to bring back their home's energy by restoring its history. Fortunately, with only three prior owners since 1888, there were many antique details that remained intact.

Puente recruited artisans familiar with old-world restoration in a range of fields from decorative plasterwork to stained glass. The Carrara marble mantels, black from use, were sanded and cleaned to their original creamy white. Casts were made of the existing plasterwork so that the missing portions could be filled in with exact copies. Wood shutters, which had long ago ceased to operate, were taken apart, stripped, and reassembled. A set of doors was found in the basement with antique hardware, which was polished and used upstairs. "It was almost obsessive," says Puente, who personally cleaned, with a mixture of vinegar and water, each crystal on the large Victorian chandeliers that came with the house.

LEFT: The garden-floor kitchen has white-lacquer cabinetry, a Wolf stove, and a Carrara marble backsplash. OPPOSITE: The walls throughout the house, including the kitchen, are in Benjamin Moore's neutral Shaker Beige. A pigment print by Los Angeles artist Burton Machen hangs near the entrance to the dining room.

The garden behind the house was overgrown with weeds. When Edge and Puente cleaned out the plants they discovered a symmetrical brick pattern underneath. Time had caused the bricks to shift and tilt, so they were removed and relaid in exactly the same design. The simple patio is now home to a five-hundred-pound Buddha set atop a pedestal in the middle of the serene garden.

The focus in restoring the house was to keep the decor spare so as to highlight the home's vintage features. The walls were painted in warm neutrals. The modern kitchen, located off the garden, has white lacquer Italian cabinetry, stainless steel appliances, and an island topped with an oak ledge. The original pine plank floors were patched with wood excavated from an upstairs bathroom. They are pitted and cracked, "but that's what makes it real," Puente says. "We were trying to keep the design as simple as possible to show them off."

The most self-consciously Zen space in the house—apart from the meditation room—has to be the striking master bathroom, which occupies an entire former bedroom. Here, both the walls and the floor were covered in French limestone. A roomy bathtub is encased in a birch surround, and a double sink is in black marble. And if that weren't enough, the room also contains one of the home's fireplaces, whose flue they restored, and a view of the backyard.

By keeping the kitchen on the ground level, Edge and Puente were able to maintain the grandeur of their parlor floor, whose high-ceilinged front and back rooms are separated by neoclassical columns. The interior design in this loftlike space is sleek, a mix of midcentury and contemporary furniture warmed up with pillows in African

textiles. These are carefully balanced with more ornate decorations—a crystal chandelier original to the house hangs in the living room, a baroque mirror is placed over the mantel.

In the rear parlor, a set of worn brocade curtains was repurposed from the dining room and now hangs on understated black wood poles. They remind Edge and Puente of the previous owner, and his long and happy tenure here. Meanwhile, a newly minted brass plaque is mounted in front of the tree directly outside the house. It reads: IN LOVING MEMORY OF MR. LARRY. 1928–2004.

PREVIOUS SPREAD, LEFT: In the main entry hall the wood floors were patched with pieces salvaged from the master bathroom. RIGHT: A classical doorway with fluted columns separates the parlors.
OPPOSITE: The master bathroom has limestone floors and a bathtub with a birch surround.
ABOVE: The bedroom, with its alcove ceiling, has silk-velvet draperies suspended from Kirsch Ripplefold ceiling tracks.

HISTORY

Prior to 1885, most American homes were heated with wood- or coal-burning brick fireplaces, or Benjamin Franklin's invention, the cast-iron stove. But while utilitarian in function, the fireplace and its mantel quickly became a vehicle that represented both a town home's architectural style as well as its owner's social status. Even after the introduction of a new amenity—central heating—the fireplace remained the focal point of any well-appointed room.

MANTEL STYLE GUIDE In colonial row houses, fireplaces were generally brick with painted wooden mantels, the fancier ones embellished with picture moldings and pedimented tops copied from European pattern books. By the Federal period, mantels had become much more ornamental, with plain or fluted columns and oval sunburst motifs and other decoration inspired by the eighteenth-century English architects Robert and James Adam. Greek Revival mantels were suitably classical and often constructed out of black marble with white or cream veining. After the Civil War, central heating came into fashion with the invention of inexpensive cast-iron radiators and steel coal furnaces. Even so, the High Victorian mantel spared no flourish, from towers and columns to bibelot (trinket) shelves and beveled mirrors. Another common late nineteenth-century mantel—a less expensive option in its day—was bluestone or slate with a faux marblized finish. It can be hard to tell this type from the real thing: try peeking under the mantel's shelf—the underside rarely got painted.

CLEANING A MARBLE MANTEL The iconic brownstone mantel is the arched keystone style made of Italian Carrara, a white marble with gray veins. These were ordered out of catalogs and arrived on-site like chunky marble puzzles, with each piece numbered. The marble tends to darken from soot and smoke: use a stiff bristle brush with mild soap and water to dislodge some of the dirt. A marble restorer can return a Carrara mantel to its original snowy white finish.

FIREPLACE SAFETY Get your chimneys and fireplaces inspected—preferably before you buy the house. Don't just go with the house inspector's report. The best way is to hire a certified chimney inspector and ask for a Level 2 inspection—this is a thorough video inspection via closed-circuit cameras of the inside of a chimney flue to check that it is properly lined and safe for burning solid fuel. Have the flue reinspected once a year and cleaned to prevent chimney fires caused by the buildup of creosote. To find a reputable chimney sweep and inspector, contact the

Chimney Safety Institute of America (see Where to Find It, page 270) for a recommendation in your neighborhood.

RELINING A CHIMNEY Many old town house chimneys are pure brick and have never been lined. If that is the case, or if cracks have developed in the lining, the chimney may need to be relined with clay tile, stainless steel liners, or poured cement. One of the best ways is to have the flue relined with cast-in-place lightweight concrete. In this wet process, the ultralight concrete is pumped into the chimney via a rubber balloon, creating a heat-proof, insulated liner. The drawback is the price—about $100,000 for a typical town house. A far less expensive alternative ($2,000–$10,000 depending on chimney height) is to insert a flexible stainless steel liner, which bends like a Slinky as it moves up a chimney flue.

CONVERTING COAL TO WOOD One reason a fireplace may be leeching smoke is that it may not have been designed for burning wood. Although early fireplaces used firewood, from the late 1820s coal was the preferred fuel in urban areas, and fireplaces were designed with smaller openings that were fitted with boxes for burning coal. That coal, by the way, was a soft variety known as cannel, which when burned smelled like rotten eggs. If your fireplace still has a coal insert, retrofit it for burning wood (or convert it to gas fire) with an arched insert by a firm such as Stovax (see Where to Find It, page 270).

REOPENING A FIREPLACE To reopen a nonworking fireplace or sealed chimney, have an expert inspect the chimney to make sure it can accommodate a working flue. Although a flue might once have been connected to a fireplace, it might have since been adapted to other purposes, such as venting the building's furnace, or accommodating

pipes and electrical work. Often homeowners discover old hearths during the course of their renovations. To bring them back to life, remember to replace the hearth extension that protects the fireplace from the room's floor, and add an arched firebox insert. Finally, make sure that the flue is properly lined.

CREATING A DRAFT Realize that if the flue is too narrow—and it often is—there is only so much you can do to improve your chimney's draft. In general, the taller the chimney, the better the draft, which is why fireplaces on the bottom floors of a building tend to work more efficiently than those higher up. Extreme temperature variations also make chimneys more efficient; the hotter the fire, and the colder the day, the better the chimney will draft. Another option for a shallow fireplace is to use a manufactured log such as a Duraflame, whose low-moisture content makes it burn hotter than a log, and position it at the back of the firebox.

THE EDWARDIAN

Date built: 1905 | Width: 30 feet | Stories: 3 | Square footage: 2,400 | Bedrooms: 4 | Fireplaces: 4
Year purchased: 1989 | Length of renovation: 2 years plus (4 years later) an additional 4 months
House style: Edwardian

San Francisco is renowned for its Painted Ladies, the colorful row houses that line the city's streets like eccentric aunts at a hillside tea party. Some 48,000 wooden houses, made mostly of then-bountiful California redwood, were built in San Francisco between the gold rush and the Panama Pacific Exhibition of 1915. Their architectural exuberance owes to the Victorian fashion for decoration, as well as to technology: the invention of the steam-powered saw in the 1830s allowed for wood to be bent, stamped, and curved into all manner of exotic shapes.

The best known of the city's Victorians are certainly dripping in ornament, from the gingerbread flourishes and rounded turrets of those in the Queen Anne style to the oddly

RIGHT: The dining room retains its original brick fireplace. OPPOSITE: In the light-filled kitchen, old-fashioned cupboards were replaced with floating shelves custom fabricated by San Francisco's Fine by Design. The island's honed marble top is an optical illusion: the three-inch facing at the edges makes it look thicker than it actually is. Above the farmhouse sink, windows face out to the garden.

shaped pediments and enormous keystones of those in the Stick-Eastlake tradition. But there is another type of wooden town house in the city, one that many connoisseurs seek out for its sparer lines and spacious layouts. The city's Edwardian homes were named for Queen Victoria's son and built during his reign (1901–1910). What they lacked in pizzazz, they gained in classical proportion. For stuffy parlors and dark skinny halls, the Edwardians substituted spacious layouts that suited their obsession with health and fresh air.

Built in 1905, this handsome Edwardian was fortunate to have survived the devastating San Francisco earthquake and fire of 1906. The house is located on a quiet street in Ashbury Heights, a romantic and tranquil neighborhood in the hills above San Francisco's more raucous Haight-Ashbury. The current owners, both top executives at Williams-Sonoma, were seduced by the home's airy layout, as well as by the view from the third-floor bedroom window, where the fog can be seen rolling in from the ocean.

They bought the town house from an architect couple who had purchased it in the 1970s, after it had been converted, like so many other of the city's row homes, into apartments. At the time, the building's wood clapboard had been replaced with metal siding. The architects set out to restore the exterior and were lucky to find copies of the original architectural plans for the house. It turned out that their town house's humble facade had originally sported a pair of twenty-foot neoclassical columns. They couldn't resist resurrecting the front in all its grandeur, re-creating the original plaster columns in longer-lasting fiberglass. They also discarded the metal siding and had the house resurfaced with wood clapboard.

The architects converted the building back into a private residence consisting of a main house of 1,800 square feet, and an additional apartment on the street level.

The money ran out before they tackled much of the interior restoration, and the house was sold to the current owners, who bought it in 1989. They lived there for five years without making many changes, then kept the house when their work took them to New York, where they lived for a decade. During that time, a niece lived in the apartment downstairs while the upstairs floors remained empty. The couple, Patrick Wade and Dave DeMattei, would visit their town house occasionally but found it disconcertingly spooky. "There were mice crawling around, windows rattling, and wind blowing through the rooms," Wade says.

When their jobs brought them back to San Francisco, they embarked on a serious renovation of the town house that lasted for four months. The drafty windows were replaced with custom-made leaded and beveled ones, the roof was replaced, and the rotted interior staircase was rebuilt. In the back garden, the patio was relined with new stone. Inside, French doors were installed, the bathrooms remodeled, and the kitchen modernized with state-of-the-art equipment along with a traditional farmhouse sink and marble-topped island.

Sometimes updating an old town house leads to hard choices. As much as the owners loved the dining room's original redwood paneling and mantel, for example, they rarely used the room because it felt dark and unappealing. "I used to run through the room, it felt so haunted," Wade says. He felt they had no choice but to lighten the paneling with glossy cream lacquer. Not wanting to lose the detail of the intricate dentil work on the mantel, Wade came up with the idea of brightening it with cream-colored spray paint. Now the pale walls are set off by their collection of blue-and-white antique transferware, displayed on a shelf that runs the length of the room.

Apart from painting the redwood details, many of the town house's other graceful notes were lovingly preserved. The living room's bay windows—a signature feature of Edwardian town houses—retain their original built-in love seats, now freshened up with tan cushions and zebra-patterned throw pillows. The master bedroom, with its view straight out to the ocean, still has its unusual green marble fireplace and a pair of bookshelves tucked into arching coves. Throughout the house, artwork is hung as it was originally intended from brass gallery rods the owners had custom-made to suspend from the wall moldings.

The columned exterior attracts attention for its stylized front garden featuring matching magnolias and symmetrical demilune boxwood hedges. But the facade, in true Edwardian fashion, is painted a restrained butter yellow—more serious uncle (with a taste for the classics) than color-mad Victorian aunt.

PREVIOUS SPREAD, LEFT: The large entry hall is dressed with raffia wallpaper and an antique table set with silver accessories and an antique ginger jar. RIGHT: The dining room's redwood paneling, original to the house, was lightened with cream lacquer paint.
OPPOSITE: The living room has its original bay windows with built-in love seats. ABOVE LEFT: A bamboo window shade filters light into a tiny powder room. ABOVE: Living room walls in Benjamin Moore's Classic Brown demonstrate that dark colors can be dramatic, not dreary, in a town house.

TOP LEFT: The master bathroom, though completely remodeled, has a classic look. BOTTOM LEFT: New French doors bring light into a guest bedroom. ABOVE: For the artful owners, every surface provides an opportunity for an interesting vignette. OPPOSITE: The shady back garden has trellised walls and irregular stone pavers.

RESTORATION NOTES WOOD SHINGLES

Warm in winter, cool in summer, wood breathes and is the ultimate green building material. A favorite cladding for town houses since colonial times, in some places—such as New Orleans or San Francisco— wood clapboard or shingle is the predominant town house facade.

HISTORY

The word *clapboard* comes from the Dutch word *klappen*, "to split," because the planks used to be hand split from logs of white pine, hemlock, spruce, or cypress. The earliest American row houses were covered in flat and undecorated clapboard, a siding of long boards (twelve inches wide in the eighteenth century) applied horizontally and overlapping on a house. By the nineteenth century, clapboards began to be sawed and were narrowed to four to six inches in width and sometimes embellished with grooves or "beads." Wood shingles came into fashion in the late 1800s, when power tools and mass production made it easy to create decorative patterns and shapes such as squares, diamonds, and hexagons.

START WITH STRUCTURE "A wood house moves a lot more than people think," says Chris Yerke, a contractor and owner of San Francisco's Restoration Workshop. "Joints come open. There can be water damage and bugs. Issue number one is making sure your roof and shell are tight." Once the structural concerns are addressed, you can move on to aesthetic concerns like repairing ornamental woodwork or repainting.

REPAIRING AND MAINTAINING Wood siding needs to be caulked and repainted every seven years or so, depending on conditions, or every three to five years if it is stained. The wood should be power washed and dried before the seal is applied.

The New York City Landmarks Preservation Commission provides this rule of thumb: if more than 50 percent of a given area of wood siding or ornament is deteriorated beyond repair, replace the whole thing. With shingles, each damaged piece should be replaced in its entirety. This is in contrast to clapboard siding, which can be repaired by replacing just the deteriorated sections.

CANADIAN GOTHIC

|GOLDEN SQUARE MILE, MONTREAL|

Date built: 1920 | Width: 26 feet | Stories: 3 | Square footage: 5,000 | Bedrooms: 5 | Fireplaces: 4
Year purchased: 2005 | Length of renovation: 1 year | House style: Tudor Gothic

In her book *O Canada*, the writer Jan Morris describes peering into the window of one of the lovely late-nineteenth-century town houses that surround Montreal's St. Louis Square. To her, the scene was quintessentially French Canadian: "so snug, so heavy with lamps and pictures, so velvety-looking in the twilight."

It's a romantic image that is redolent of the architecture of Montreal. From the humble row houses of the Plateau Mont-Royal, where Leonard Cohen owns a small home, to the elegant gray stone town houses of the city center, these historic houses are essential to the city's texture and scale. So much so that when entire neighborhoods of them were threatened by development, the architect Phyllis Lambert, made saving the row houses of Montreal one of her first preservationist crusades.

PREVIOUS SPREAD, LEFT: The dining room's original mahogany-paneled walls were stripped of several layers of paint. The wing chair, upholstered in a fabric patterned with classical urns, is the work of interior designer Scott Yetman. RIGHT: A persimmon carpet brightens the staircase in the entry hall. OPPOSITE: Built in the Tudor Gothic style, the home's living room has a coffered ceiling.

The young couple who purchased this Tudor Gothic brick town house on Mountain Street in the shadow of Mount Royal had no intention of turning it into an homage to the fin de siècle. The wife, trained as an architect, wanted a house with enough conveniences for a family that included three small children. But she and her husband had an appreciation for architectural history. What she got was a home that literally creaked with it.

Built in 1920, the town house was designed by Robert Findlay, a Scottish-born architect of several important buildings in Montreal, including the Westmount Public Library and the Sun Life Assurance Company head office. He also designed many residences in the city. This one, known as the Jules Hamel House, had a Gothic feel, from the pointed-arch leaded windows in front to the stone fireplace and coffered ceiling in the living room. Perhaps that is why the Anglican Church acquired the property in the 1960s as a residence for the bishop of Montreal. The current owners bought it from the church in 2005. "What's nice is that everything's original," says Scott Yetman, the interior designer who worked with the couple on the renovation. "It had never been 'wonderfully' renovated. But it had never been ignored either."

LEFT: Plaster Corinthian-style columns leading into the dining room were painted to look like stone. The pillars, along with the living room's painted-arch stone fireplace (above), add to the Gothic feel. OPPOSITE: In the dining room, the built-in cabinetry has leaded windows and is filled with cut-crystal glassware that came with the house. The antique bronze chandelier is French.

The wife had admired the house for years, ever since she and her future husband had paid a visit to the bishop, who was to officiate at their wedding. "We knew it was a great house, but when it came on the market we weren't sure it would work for us," she says. "We needed another bedroom, and the kitchen was too dark. We thought about how to fix it but it was a puzzle."

They solved it with the help of Montreal architect Todd Richards. He noticed that the house had a garage addition that blocked light from entering the back of the house. The solution was to excavate and lower the garage to make way for a new and larger addition that would accommodate a bright new kitchen and a bedroom on an upper floor.

Like many people who alter a historic town house, the homeowners faced a quandary. Should the addition try to replicate the original architecture, or should they renovate the older sections of the house in an attempt to fuse the two parts? They decided to faithfully restore the old while letting the newer parts look clearly modern—in effect to have two houses in one. What makes it work are the thoughtful connections between the two. The materials used for the new addition—redbrick, leaded windows, copper flashings—have clear stylistic echoes in the front of the house. The kitchen's new ceiling has a square coffered pattern, reminiscent of the much older one in the living room.

OPPOSITE: The kitchen is located in a new addition to the house whose architecture complements the older section. The white ceiling, like that in the living room, is coffered. The mahogany counters add warmth and allude to the dining room's antique paneling. ABOVE: A Spanish-style table, which also came with the house, has white chairs by Thomas O'Brien, and a banquette in faux blue leather.

They emphasized the theatricality of the older rooms in the house while tweaking them with a combination of antique and modern furnishings. In the living room, which has an almost medieval quality, Yetman stripped the paint off the oak panels surrounding the carved stone fireplace and covered the room's twisted plaster columns in faux-stone decorative paint. The Dutch bronze chandelier that came with the house stayed in situ, but it is now joined by more modern furnishings, like a limed-oak coffee table and a pair of life-size painted silhouettes by the Quebec artist Luc Bergeron.

The dining room's eclecticism perfectly illustrates the owners' decorating philosophy. The mahogany-paneled walls, which had been painted, were restored and varnished and hung with a wide-ranging art collection, from antique family portraits to contemporary art. Instead of an antique dining table, they chose a more up-to-date X-shaped design in ebonized wood.

The dining room also contains Yetman's favorite vignette: an antique painting of a somber Scotsman hangs over an elaborate japanned lacquer console from turn-of-the-century France (see page 193, bottom right). For anyone familiar with Montreal's cultural history, with its dual—and sometimes dueling—French and English heritage, the juxtaposition is bound to elicit a smile. Or as Yetman put it: "I'm sure the Scottish ancestor in that portrait would never have allowed such a wild piece of furniture in his house."

ABOVE: The master bedroom, painted a warm apricot-yellow, is filled with original architectural details, including an arched window, a classical fireplace, wall moldings, and a coved ceiling.
OPPOSITE: The rear of the house, while all new, mimics the facade, with its red brick masonry, leaded windows, and stone insets. A copper roof provides shade from the sun in summer and protection from the snow in winter.

SIMPLY FRENCH

|BROOKLYN HEIGHTS, BROOKLYN|

Date built: Circa 1830 | Width: 25 feet | Stories: 4 | Square footage: 3,800 | Bedrooms: 6 | Fireplaces: 7
Year purchased: 2003 | Length of renovation: 12 months | House style: Federal

Anne Attal never planned to buy a historic New York City town house. Though she had grown up in old houses in the French Normandy countryside, this mother of three young children was now separating from her husband and envisioned shaking off her past by moving into a modern loft. "My life was complicated," Attal says. "I wanted something peaceful and Zen. Old houses felt old-fashioned, but when I saw this house I changed my mind."

The house was a four-story, twenty-five-foot-wide Federal-style home that she learned had been designed and built by a Swedish shipbuilder for his family. She liked the proportions of the house, with its square rooms and light that reaches from one side of the house to the other. The house's Scandinavian pedigree also resonated with Attal. She had always appreciated

ABOVE: Attal found the living room's black marble mantel too shiny for her taste and had it sanded to a matte finish. OPPOSITE: On the parlor floor, blue-gray doorframes in Benjamin Moore's Nantucket Fog add architectural definition to the mostly white color scheme inspired by traditional Swedish interiors. The floors were painted with patio enamel.

the simplicity of Swedish country decorating, with its serene furnishings and cool palette of blues, greens, and creamy whites.

The town house had never been extensively renovated, which proved both a blessing and a curse. On the positive side, it was brimming with original features, such as fireplace mantels, doorknobs, and what Attal believes is the original front door lock and key. On the other hand, the building required an extensive renovation. The roof was replaced and the windows taken apart and rebuilt. The house had been advertised as having seven fireplaces, but not one was in working order. Attal had three fireplace flues relined to make them functional.

The biggest decision was how to modernize the kitchens and bathrooms without intruding on the square symmetry that had attracted her to the house. Aesthetics won out over convenience. She did not enlarge the tiny bathrooms, which were tucked onto hallway landings, but she did freshen them up with quaint French touches like wire shelves and soap holders. The biggest decision for an accomplished cook like Attal was where to put the kitchen. It was originally on the ground level, but Attal had rented out that floor as an apartment. Eschewing the trend for sprawling modern kitchens, she turned the sunroom off the back dining room into a miniature, shipshape galley with open shelving, cement-tile floors, and high-end appliances concealed behind mismatched wooden cabinetry. With storage space at a minimum,

OPPOSITE: The dining room's French doors lead to a sunroom that has been converted into a kitchen. The budget decor includes a mix of Mexican dining table, Ikea chairs, and a candelabra from Anthropologie. ABOVE: The living room is furnished with pieces Attal has collected over the years, including an Indian armoire, a white loveseat, and a chaise.

she sold off her formal dishes and small electrical appliances at a stoop sale, the Brooklyn equivalent of a yard sale. Today she makes do with a single set of white plates and a stovetop espresso maker.

Attal furnished the house on a budget, striving for a Swedish look "with zero Swedish furniture." She ordered simple white-slipcovered pieces from catalogs and mixed them with inherited European antiques such as her ex-husband's great-grandmother's bed and armoire from the north of France. The color scheme is deceptively simple, with ceilings painted in lighter shades of white than walls, and doors and window frames in stronger colors for definition. "It doesn't look like it but there are fifty-nine colors in this house," she says.

Her favorite room in the house is the starkest: her all-white bedroom, with its painted floor, fireplace, and a rosary hung (with a little tongue in cheek) above her iron bed. The room, which faces the backyard, gets very little street noise and achieves the absolute calm that Attal is seeking. "Life is getting so cluttered," she says. "I'm done with knickknacks. More and more, I am drawn to this idea of living simply."

OPPOSITE: The kitchen's rustic decor is based on French country style. Attal deliberately mixed woods like mahogany and oak for cabinet fronts. A cooktop is built into a maple butcher-block counter. ABOVE: Attal collects vintage French café-au-lait bowls and other kitchen artifacts. TOP RIGHT: The farmhouse sink is by the French firm Villeroy & Boch. RIGHT: The dining room's window, formerly on the rear facade, now opens onto the kitchen. Attal's daughter Nina, with dog Rice, perches on the sill while she prepares lunch in the background.

PREVIOUS SPREAD, LEFT: Carpenter Roy Glorioso lined the small study with floor-to-ceiling wooden shelves. RIGHT: The guest bedroom has lavender walls and a yellow ceiling. The bed and armoire are family heirlooms from France.

OPPOSITE: "I wanted the most peaceful bedroom possible," Attal says. The iron bed is from Charles P. Rogers Beds, while the rosary was purchased at a yard sale. ABOVE: Her daughter Nina's bedroom has vintage wallpaper deliberately applied in patches. LEFT: In the master bedroom, the mantel is arranged with family photos. "It's very feng shui to have pictures of people you love where you sleep," Attal says.

In most historic homes, a window's surrounding details, such as the window sash and framing, were designed to harmonize with the overall architecture. Any alteration to the original design will usually look off—which is why local preservation agencies are such sticklers for historically correct windows. One of the biggest decisions a homeowner will have to make is whether to repair the old windows or have them replaced.

HISTORY

A window gets its character from the details of its design: the ornamentation surrounding the sashes, or panels, that allow the window to be opened and closed, and the number of glass panes (or "lights") the window holds, each one separated by narrow muntins. In the colonial period, all glass was handblown, so it was impossible to make large panes: this is why eighteenth-century windows in America often had twelve-over-twelve panes separated by muntins. As glassmaking methods improved, larger panes were possible and preferable because of the light they afforded. By the nineteenth century, two-over-two or one-over-one windows were the norm for row houses. (A subtle detail that makes all the difference: in historic windows, the panes were always rectangular and vertical.) Metal windows were rarely used until the 1930s.

REHABBING OLD WINDOWS If your building still has its historic windows, consider having them repaired rather than replaced. Sometimes it's just a matter of removing more than a century's worth of accumulated paint, and replacing only the severely damaged sections. Consider that most historic windows are made of old-growth lumber, which is highly rot resistant; new wood windows are generally made of recently harvested pine lumber that is highly porous. As Clem Labine, founder of *Old-House Journal* notes, the old-fashioned window balance system—in which ropes, chains, and pulleys are balanced with counterweights—is reliable and easy to fix. "If something breaks, you just put in a new sash cord or chain," he says, "whereas with new windows the mechanisms often become obsolete and there is usually no way to repair or replace them." If properly maintained, a wood window can last more than two hundred years. For added insulation, storm windows can be installed: look for "invisible" storms, which disappear into a window's opening.

REPLACING WINDOWS It is not always possible to save old windows. Some have rotted beyond the point of repair. In many cases, a home's historic windows are long gone, replaced with aluminum. Old windows can also be drafty, particularly if you don't add storm windows in winter. For greater energy efficiency, modern options for windows include Low-E glass, in which argon gas is sandwiched between panes to reduce heat loss, and laminated safety glass, which can protect your interior from ultraviolet damage and dampen noise. For great aesthetic appeal, major window manufacturers such as Marvin have begun to offer replacement windows that look historic and will pass inspections in landmark districts. Only a handful of custom window makers offer true old-fashioned weight-and-chain windows. These include New York–based Zeluck, Inc. and Architectural Windows and Entries (see Where to Find It, page 270). As Roy Zeluck—the third-generation president of Zeluck, Inc.—notes, even "in an antiquated industry, there have been advances," adding that more and more clients are requesting soundproof glazing and childproof window hardware.

GHOST STORY

|HISTORIC DISTRICT, SAVANNAH|

Date built: 1849–85 | Width: 25 feet | Stories: 4 | Square footage: 6,000 | Bedrooms: 4 | Fireplaces: 8
Year purchased: 2006 | Length of renovation: 6 months | House style: Greek Revival

When Ronald and Lisa Mahoney Oliver purchased their Savannah town house, they quickly discovered that in addition to its eight fireplaces and extra-wide entrance hall, the house was equipped with an amenity not listed in the sales contract: a ghost. They heard about their other-worldly visitor from neighbors, then unearthed a 1960 article in the *Savannah Morning News* that told the tale of a Yankee soldier who was shot during the Civil War right outside the three-story brick town house in the city's historic district. The homeowners took pity on the soldier and brought him inside to die in comfort. "The grateful young soldier likes it so well, he returns at unexpected times to visit," the article stated.

PREVIOUS SPREAD, LEFT: The kitchen has an original fireplace and bright red custom cabinetry. ABOVE: An Irish Georgian console adds an elegant touch to the entrance hall. OPPOSITE: The comfortable sitting room, located in the rear parlor, is the owners' favorite place to relax.

The Olivers, who bought the town house on a whim while driving across the southern United States, can understand its mysterious draw. Ronald, who is known as Oli, is a former boat liveryman who was one of the original partners in Crocs shoes, which were originally targeted at the sailing crowd. He had recently reconnected with Lisa, a friend from two decades earlier. Neither had ever married, and they were driving through Savannah when they decided the romantic town was where they wanted to be married and set up their first home together.

A newcomer to the city, Lisa promptly hired a local decorator to help with the town house, but found her designs were much too formal for the casual elegance the Olivers were envisioning. Meanwhile, Lisa had been frequenting Arcanum, a Savannah interior design and antiques shop whose owners, Sim Harvey and Phillip Hunter, blend antique, vintage, and new pieces with sophistication and flair. She begged Harvey, who is also an interior designer, to take on a daunting assignment— not only to furnish the house in time for the marriage, just six months away, but also to plan and organize the wedding festivities.

OPPOSITE: The drawing room, or front parlor, has a formal decorating scheme in muted shades of green and brown. ABOVE: A curtain has a silver-leaf lion's-head tieback. RIGHT: A brown velvet chair is a comfortable perch beside a nickel-plated cocktail table.

Savannahians call the front parlor the drawing room, since this is the space to which women would traditionally withdraw after dinner. By the time Harvey stepped in, the room had been furnished with antiques and painted a sedate sea-foam blue. He lightened the mood with a pale patterned Oushak carpet and added unusual decorative objects like a set of hand-carved tribal shells that had been used as currency. A Georgian-style chandelier was ordered in a silver-plated finish rather than the usual brass. "It's a traditional form that nods to the history of the house, but the silver makes it modern," he says, cautioning that the fixture needs regular polishing.

The sitting room, which occupies the rear parlor, is the Olivers' favorite place in the house. The unusual palette was inspired by the colors in local artist Ann Osteen's painting *Boiled Peanut,* which hangs over the sofa. The walls are a golden brown, offset by the interiors of Regency-style alcoves that are blue-green, the edges embellished with gold leaf. This room leads to the kitchen, where Lisa ordered cabinetry made by a local firm, Black Dog Studio, in her favorite color: red.

Both the sitting room and the kitchen overlook the courtyard, one of Oli's main preoccupations. He wanted a garden that reminded him of Mexico, where he had lived off and on for a couple of years while setting up a distribution network for Crocs. He removed a muddy fishpond from the patio to create more space for plants, and filled containers with plants and trees, including a broad-leaf banana. Southern jasmine climbs up the kitchen sidewall, while fig ivy wends up the brick on the wall adjacent to the alley. Oli also had the courtyard repaved with antique Savannah gray

ABOVE: The four-poster bed helps give the small master bedroom a sense of scale, while the zebra-patterned stools add a playful twist to the traditional decor. OPPOSITE: The lavish master bathroom has white marble wainscoting and floors and a sculptural Monaco bathtub in volcanic limestone from the English firm Victoria + Albert. The wall color is Benjamin Moore's Bird's Egg.

brick, and decorated the borders with even older bricks that came to America from England on ships where they were used as ballast.

Meanwhile, on the top floor of the house, the master bedroom was designed as a soothing retreat. The walls are a cool robin's egg blue, while a four-poster bed gives definition to the medium-size bedroom. The showpiece is the bathroom, which is filled with sunlight and such luxurious fixtures as a silver-leaf mirror and a deep, glossy-white minimalist bathtub.

In Savannah, most town houses were built with a carriage house in the back. When automobiles replaced horses, many homeowners built a passageway that connected the main house to the former carriage house. This was the case at the Olivers, where an interior passageway from the kitchen leads to what is now a guest bedroom suite overlooking the garden. It's popular with all their guests, including the one who never got a formal invitation. "Oli and I have definitely seen that ghost there," Lisa says. "He has a presence."

OPPOSITE: The owners say they spotted their home's resident ghost in the carriage house, which is now connected to the main house by an interior passageway. The guest bedroom in the carriage house overlooks the courtyard (above), which was repaved with Savannah gray brick.

THE ALLEY CATS

Date built: 1790–1870 | Width: 60 feet | Stories: 3 | Square footage: 3,700 | Bedrooms: 2 | Fireplaces: 6
Year purchased: 1974–99 | Length of renovation: 20 years | House style: Federal

It takes imagination to transform a Baltimore alley lined with crumbling row houses into a Tuscan-style home complete with a Palladian-style loggia, an outdoor fireplace, antique-filled salons, and an expansive garden lush with fig trees and roses. But when the homeowners are Vincent Peranio and Dolores Deluxe, no one in their native Baltimore even blinks an eye. Peranio is the production designer who has conjured up the look and feel of his gritty hometown through his sets for directors like John Waters and Barry Levinson, and for such television shows as *Homicide: Life on the Street* and *The Wire*. Today, he lives with his wife, Deluxe, who is a set decorator, in a fanciful compound they have assembled out of what were once five adjacent alley houses in the Fells Point section of Baltimore, not far from the city's harbor.

PREVIOUS SPREAD, LEFT: The decor of the combined Baltimore alley homes is pure stagecraft, beginning with the frescoed grand entrance, also known as the Red Room.
ABOVE: In the garden, a brick exterior from the 1830s shows its age. OPPOSITE: The couple makes regular use of their vintage kitchen appliances, including a 1919 Oriole cast-iron stove and a 1929 GE Monitor Top refrigerator that needs periodic defrosting.

Baltimore is a city of row houses, from the elegant Italianates of Federal Hill to the humbler Formstone homes of working-class East Baltimore. But the smallest and least appreciated of these homes have always been the city's alley houses, which were sometimes no wider than ten to twelve feet. Built in the eighteenth and nineteenth centuries, these—Peranio explains—"were the tiniest houses in Baltimore, located off the main streets and formerly homes to ship caulkers, oyster shuckers, freed slaves, and prostitutes."

Peranio and Deluxe never planned to occupy a row of five houses. At first, Peranio could barely afford the rent on one of the homes, even though it was located in what was then one of the least expensive of the city's neighborhoods, with a crime rate to match. "It started in 1974," Peranio says. "I was an artist, and I rented one of the little houses, a two-hundred-year-old building, for fifty dollars a month. When I met Dolores, I was nine months behind in my rent."

ABOVE: A movie poster from *Female Trouble* is a memento from the set of a John Water's movie. RIGHT: Although the interiors were extensively renovated, this extremely narrow staircase, original to its 1830s structure, was left untouched. Beside it, above a vintage telephone table, are a collection of found objects that the couple calls "primitives," including antique bottles they dug up from their backyard and a can of buckshot discovered in the attic. OPPOSITE: The wood floor of the 1830s kitchen, now used as a hallway, was replaced with brick to stave off termite damage. The space, which still has its original fireplace, is filled with favorite things, from turquoise Tiffany boxes to a lamp that once belonged to Peranio's aunt, Viola.

They were soon able to buy the all-wood home for just $2,500, but when the floors began to cave in due to extensive termite damage, they were forced to move into the neighboring house, which dated from the 1830s. Twenty years later, an elderly neighbor moved, and they purchased her house. Then a fourth came up for sale, and finally the fifth, which now serves as a warehouse for their extensive collection of props. In total, the real estate cost them $70,000, a pittance today, now that the atmospheric neighborhood, which is convenient to the city's rejuvenated waterfront yet retains the feel of an eighteenth-century sailor town, has become fashionable.

Peranio and Deluxe live in three of the houses, two of which are now connected through a door in the house's main entrance, known as the Red Room. The first house, sadly, no longer exists. Condemned by the city, the building was ordered to be torn down. Peranio and Deluxe, who had hoped to keep it, reluctantly turned it into their parking pad. "I looked at it as a picturesque ruin in our garden," Peranio says. "It was covered with wisteria. But that's the romantic set designer in me."

Touring the warren of rooms that make up their living spaces, it's impossible to tell that the houses were extensively renovated. The couple, with the help of Deluxe's father, a licensed contractor and antiques dealer, stripped the buildings to their brick walls and installed new beams and, to repel termites, concrete and brick flooring.

Then they started layering in what Peranio calls "the patina"—their lifetime collection of building materials, furnishings, and found objects. A set of Victorian doors came from the set of the John Waters film *Desperate Living*. The red kitchen cabinets were left over from a Purdue chicken commercial. "When we first met," Deluxe says, "he was collecting vintage 1940s brocade and I was collecting bar cloth and chintz. We've never met a thing we couldn't develop a thing for."

While the decor inside the houses sashays from high baroque to high camp, it is the garden that is the showstopper. Once a series of cemented yards, it is now a ravishing shade garden with statuary, terraced steps, weeping cherry and dogwood trees, and a profusion of flowering plants from irises to mums. The boxwoods were from the set of *Serial Mom*.

The pièce de résistance is a full Italian loggia, complete with an outdoor fireplace and a shaded terrace, where the couple entertains friends at a long dining table. The idea came to them after a trip to Italy. "It's like coming home to a tiny resort," Peranio says. "It's a little fantasy—delusions of grandeur on a miniature scale. You could call it our personal set."

RESTORATION NOTES BRICKWORK

Bricks are wonderfully organic. Made from the earth's clay, these building blocks expand and contract with a house as the seasons change. But like wood, or any construction material with a natural basis, brickwork must be carefully maintained. Paint brick, and it can't breathe. Forget to repoint its mortar, and your interior walls will collect moisture.

HISTORY

The earliest row houses in the American colonies were built of bricks made by pressing wet clay by hand or machine into wooden molds, which were baked in the sun and then fired in kilns. Too heavy to ship, they were usually made locally, often right at the building site, which is why antique native brick—from Savannah grays to Old Chicagos—have distinct hues. When hydraulic and screw presses were invented to compress dry clay into molds, bricks became denser and perfectly regular, allowing for smooth and pristine brick facades. Most nineteenth-century mortar was a mixture of about three parts sand and one part slaked lime or crushed limestone, to which water was added. Today, most bricklayers use premixed mortars composed largely of sand, lime, and portland cement.

REPOINTING The majority of leaks in brick town houses are caused by failure in the mortar joints. When this happens, and it inevitably will, the damaged mortar will need to be cleared out and replaced in a process known as repointing. If the house's bricks are porous or were laid with a fine or decorative mortar, the repointing should be done by hand. This method is known as hand raking and involves removing the mortar with a tool called a joint raker, which has metal wheels attached to a masonry nail that neatly scrapes out the joints without damaging the brick. Hard portland cement mortar is usually removed with a grinder or a power tool equipped with a carbide blade, but this technique can result in more risk to the brick. A compromise can be to hand rake the facade but allow careful use of power tools on the side and rear of a house. When repointing, make sure the mortar matches the original. Ask the mason to do a test and let the mortar stand for a week to verify the shade when dry. Richard Marks, a Charleston restoration expert who worked on the Charleston Revival house (see page 21), recommends spritzing the wet mortar with water before it dries. This technique brings aggregates such as brick particles and crushed quartz to the surface, giving the mortar a less shiny and more weathered appearance.

PREVENTING MOISTURE DAMAGE
One telltale sign of this is a phenomenon known as efflorescence, which appears as a white powder on the bricks. This is caused by water leaching out salts and minerals as it travels through the brick and mortar and then evaporates on the surface. There are many causes, from poor construction materials to coatings, including paint and waterproof sealants, that prevent bricks from breathing as they should. Before undertaking a facade restoration, send a sample of your home's brick and mortar to an architectural conservator for analysis. The lab report will analyze the bricks' condition and recommend an appropriate and perfectly matched mortar. In very rare cases, brick can be so porous or corroded that it will need to be replaced.

REGULAR MAINTENANCE Inspect roofs, gutters, flashing, and downspouts regularly and repair as necessary. Have the mortar checked once a year for deterioration and repoint when needed. Make sure that windowsills are caulked and fixed so they don't collect water.

ROCK 'N' ROLL REVIVAL

|GREENWICH VILLAGE, NEW YORK CITY|

Date built: 1838 | Width: 25 feet | Stories: 6 | Square footage: 5,500 | Bedrooms: 4 | Fireplaces: 6
Year purchased: 2004 | Length of renovation: 7 months | House style: Greek Revival

This New York brownstone's decor—a bohemian mix of period architecture, fringed lamps, and mod wallpaper—has a quirky ambience reminiscent of the house in Wes Anderson's *The Royal Tenenbaums*. And as with the fictional Tenenbaums, here, too, there is a charismatic family in residence.

Simon Kirke is a British drummer and founder of the 1970s bands Free and Bad Company. His wife, Lorraine, who is also English, designs a fashion line, Geminola. The couple has three daughters: Domino (a pop singer) and Jemima (an artist), who no longer live at home but are frequent visitors; and Lola, a college student whose salmon bedroom has a walk-in wardrobe and hot-pink velvet sofa.

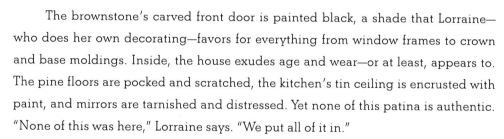

The brownstone's carved front door is painted black, a shade that Lorraine—who does her own decorating—favors for everything from window frames to crown and base moldings. Inside, the house exudes age and wear—or at least, appears to. The pine floors are pocked and scratched, the kitchen's tin ceiling is encrusted with paint, and mirrors are tarnished and distressed. Yet none of this patina is authentic. "None of this was here," Lorraine says. "We put all of it in."

In fact, the brownstone's interior had undergone numerous renovations over the course of its life, but Kirke felt it had lost its character and passed on it. To her eye, she says, it had been overrenovated—"the most formal thing I'd ever seen." Three years later, she heard that it was still on the market. This time she visited it in springtime. The magnolia tree behind the house was dripping with loose pink blossoms. As she sat in the garden in the rear, she realized she could bring the house back.

For her fashion line, Lorraine recycles vintage clothing into new garments; her creations are quite popular, with a following among stars like Nicole Kidman and Sarah Jessica Parker. She takes the old clothes apart, redyes them, and reassembles them into entirely new creations. She approaches the interior design of her home

ABOVE: In the living room, Kirke used black paint to highlight the frames of the brownstone's original fifteen-paned windows. The eclectic decor is a mix of vintage Fortuny fabrics, tufted ottomans, and fringed lamps. OPPOSITE: The master suite (left), including this room-sized bathing boudoir, occupies the entire third floor. An eclectic mix of art and antiques greets visitors in the home's main entrance hall (right).

in much the same way. She is constantly scouring antique stores and flea markets for antique building materials—even diving into Dumpsters around her neighborhood if there are interesting remnants to be had. These finds, from old shutters to fragments of glass and wall trim, are repurposed as anything from bookcases to bathroom vanities.

Lorraine had admired the design of two New York restaurants, Pastis and Balthazar, whose interiors cleverly simulate the look of weathered Parisian brasseries. She approached the architect of those spaces, Richard Lewis, to help with her house. It wasn't always an easy collaboration. Lorraine admits that her approach is chaotic: she designs each space as she goes, often inspired by the find of the day, whether it's a set of metal doors, or some rusted old railings. "It was pretty intense," Lewis says. "She would go out and buy things and we would make them work. There was

a lot of engineering that went into each decision."

For Lewis, the key to realizing Lorraine's vision was finding artisans who could understand and interpret her ideas. Robert Padilla, a decorative painter who had worked with Lewis on the restaurants, left no inch of the house untouched. One would never know that most of the pine floors are new; Padilla aged them, using a complicated process of applying chemicals and stains. The home's unusual color scheme—bubble gum–tinted hallways, turquoise ceilings, and glazed walls in yellow and Bordeaux red—was all custom mixed on his palette.

Lorraine had gone through several carpenters, none of whom were on her wavelength, before she met the furniture maker Thomas Muchowski. She first gave him a tryout, handing him a pile of wood scraps and drawers and asking him to transform them into a bed for a downstairs apartment. His jewel box of a creation, a three-walled bed that feels like its own tiny room, won her over with its ingenuity and artfulness. Soon, he set to work piecing together the elaborate kitchen, with its intricate millwork and bookcase-framed entries, and an even more fanciful bed for her youngest daughter's bedroom upstairs.

If minimalism has an opposite, it's the decor of this house. The rooms have

The Kirke's youngest daughter was the last of
the three sisters to be living at home when her
parents bought the town house. Her expansive
upstairs bedroom, painted Venetian pink, has
its own bathroom and walk-in closet (above).
Her bed is set within an alcove fashioned
out of vintage wood scraps and architectural
ornaments, in a one-of-a-kind confection built by
Muchowski (right).

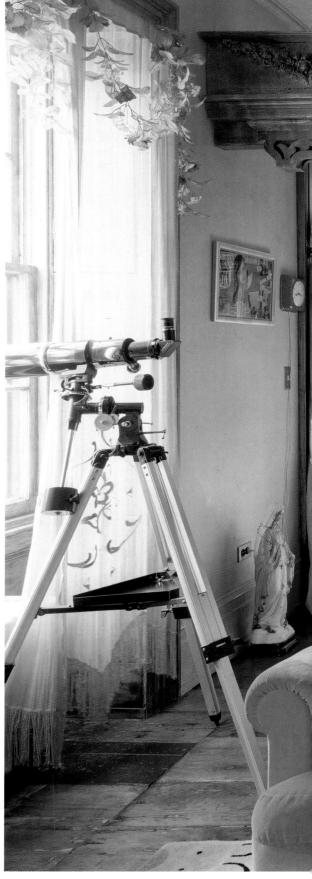

PREVIOUS SPREAD, LEFT: Kirke's charming bathrooms are designed as retreats from the chaos of their busy household. "Where else do you go when you want to have a good cry?" she says. In the master bedroom, a shower room has vintage 1960s wallpaper from Secondhand Rose in New York City and an antique mirrored console retrofitted with a dentist's sink. RIGHT: A guest bathroom has an antique bathtub and vintage floral linoleum, also from Secondhand Rose.

ABOVE: The ground floor has a separate apartment that was initially created for one of their daughters. The kitchen has striped linoleum, a miniature vintage stove, and a cabinet that conceals a fold-out kitchen table. RIGHT: The apartment's handmade alcove bed has built-in shelves for books and a velvet curtain for privacy. OPPOSITE: The rear garden, designed by Miranda Brooks, has gravel walks and a pergola.

multiple layers of pattern and decoration, from the tufted English ottomans to the slightly threadbare curtains in vintage Fortuny fabric in the living room. There are chandeliers and lamps everywhere, though as Lorraine points out, the light they cast is deliberately dim. Most of all, there is art everywhere, from important artists including Alice Neel and Robert Longo, to drawings by the Kirkes' daughter Jemima. Nothing quite matches, and to Lorraine, that is the point. "I have friends who talk about buying a couch forever," she says. "I don't understand that mentality. A house is a home, not a showpiece. It's a bit like life—it falls into place."

RESTORATION NOTES SALVAGE

Architectural antiques—commonly known as salvage—have become a big business. It's all out there, from doors to chandelier parts. Start your search with local dealers, since they are the likeliest to have the closest matches—a mantel from marble extracted from a nearby quarry, or millwork in the same wood as your banister. Search the Internet or your local phone book under antiques, salvage, junk, or demolition contractors. A wonderful sourcebook is the annual *Guide to Architectural Salvage and Antique Lumber Companies* (see Where to Find It, page 270). Your own house might be a gold mine of hidden architectural antiques. Cabinetry and mantels are sometimes buried behind false walls, and vintage hardware hidden under layers of paint. Here are tips on tracking down recycled materials for your home:

LIGHTING Homeowners can get lucky and sometimes find their home's original chandeliers intact or packed away in the attic or basement. Antique lighting specialists can rewire an old lamp. Cleaning an old chandelier is a painstaking project: the lamp must be taken apart, each piece cleaned, and the metal scrubbed with polish. Replacement parts can be tracked down through lighting dealers and specialists (see Where to Find It, page 270).

MILLWORK Salvage and antique dealers can supply everything from moldings and baluster ends to such major pieces as pier mirrors and doors. It's worth tracking down antique woodwork, as it was often created from old-growth lumber, which is both beautifully grained and harder—and therefore more long lasting—than most new wood.

PLUMBING FIXTURES Old sinks and bathtubs (especially claw-foot tubs) are easy to

find, as are reproductions made from the same molds. Be aware that the spread between the hot- and cold-water faucets has changed over the years; try to find fixtures with the fittings intact. Antique tubs in good condition are especially valuable, as they were fired with long-lasting porcelain glazes baked at up to 2,000 degrees, a toxic process no longer permitted by the EPA. Cracked porcelain can be refinished with a chemical glaze, but this finish will last only a few years. Try to remove

stains with a cleanser such as Comet or CLR. Be aware that some building codes prohibit the use of old toilets. Antique radiators are another good find as long as they are not cracked. Have a painted radiator stripped so the pipes and valves are clean.

HARDWARE In an old house, even the hinges can be valuable antiques. Dealers can provide hinges, bolts, switch plates, doorknobs, drawer pulls, hooks, house numbers, door fixtures, bell buttons, casement fasteners, heat registers, latches, and catches.

In terms of finish, polished brass was popular with the Victorians (many of whom had servants to polish it); today brass can be lacquered, requiring no polishing. Try soaking it in nontoxic wood stripper overnight in a Ziploc bag. If the piece is too rusted, companies like Al Bar Wilmette Platers in Wilmette, Illinois, can clean and polish it to like-new condition.

RECLAIMED STONE, TILE, AND BRICK Recycled construction materials such as stone and brick not only look good, but they are also a greener way to build. Architectural salvage yards are a good source of antique stone, vintage tile, and brick for building or landscaping. Innovative nonprofit groups like Build It Green! NYC are another place to check for materials; their goal is to encourage recycling by providing salvaged materials at low cost.

ALL IN THE FAMILY

|PARK SLOPE, BROOKLYN|

Date built: 1886 | Width: 20 feet | Stories: 5 | Square footage: 4,100 | Bedrooms: 5 | Fireplaces: 6
Year purchased: 2004 | Length of renovation: 9 months | House style: Italianate

In the late nineteenth century, row houses in upper-middle-class neighborhoods were routinely decorated with fine finishes and elaborate cabinetry in carved mahogany. The woodwork, when intact, is gorgeous, but it can also feel heavy and old-fashioned, at odds with the modern families now living with it. But paint that mahogany white? Or pull the cabinetry out? That seems like a sacrilege.

The homeowners of this Brooklyn brownstone came up with an elegant solution. Rather than demolish the room's mahogany vitrines, they retrofitted them with glass shelves and halogen lighting, turning their back parlor into an open-plan kitchen. Two cabinet doors were removed to make way for a stainless-steel refrigerator and an appliance hutch. The back wall

was lined with antique subway tiles (recycled from an upstairs bathroom) and set in black grout, to make it looked aged.

The kitchen belongs to Chris Mitchell, a magazine publisher, and his wife, Pilar Guzmán, an editor. But there is another intriguing aspect of the restoration: Chris and his brother, Gregg, bought and renovated the brownstone together. In fact, in Brooklyn and many other cities, spacious town houses have long sheltered extended families (not to mention, in the early years especially, the household staff).

For the brothers, the idea of living together as adults began in jest. Chris and Pilar had just had their first son, Henry, and were living in Manhattan. Gregg, a vice president of Bennison Fabrics, was married to a photographer, Andrea Chu. New York City real estate prices had become exorbitant, and the two couples kidded about moving in together. Gradually the idea became less far-fetched, and they set out to buy a Brooklyn brownstone. One March weekend, with a snowstorm swirling outside, Chris, Gregg, and Andrea visited the first house on their list, an 1886 Victorian in Park Slope, a brownstone-laden neighborhood filled with great schools, hardware stores, pizza joints, and bistros.

PREVIOUS SPREAD, LEFT: Rather than remove a leftover doorframe, the shallow space was preserved and made into a cozy alcove.
OPPOSITE: The house is a trove of late nineteenth-century millwork, including the entry hall's large mahogany hall tree, complete with a bench and hooks for hanging your hat.
ABOVE: The front parlor, which serves as a combined living and dining room, has a floor-to-ceiling Victorian console mirror that contrasts with more modern touches like a dining table from BDDW and a set of Hans Wegner Wishbone chairs.

ABOVE: In the kitchen, the parlor's fireplace was converted to gas. A portrait purchased at a flea market hangs overhead. RIGHT: Rather than remove the rear parlor's elaborate carved-wood cabinetry, the owners retrofitted it with glass shelving and halogen lighting, and incorporated it into their kitchen design. The back wall was lined in antique subway tile repurposed from the second floor bathroom, while the kitchen island has a walnut base and a Carrara marble countertop. OPPOSITE: Original mahogany pocket doors separate the two parlors.

It was an estate sale, and everything in the house needed updating, from the wiring to the plumbing, but it had the thing they most valued: character. "It had this cinematic quality," Chris says. "I could picture coming home from work on a winter's night and the kids running down the stairs to greet me. Because of the blizzard, Pilar had stayed home with the baby, but she came quickly to see it and happily consented to the purchase."

The first task was to draw up some kind of financial arrangement. They thought about splitting the house into two legally separate apartments, such as in a cooperative housing arrangement, but they decided the brownstone had more value as a single-family home. Chris and Pilar would occupy the top three floors, while Gregg and Andrea would live in the bottom floor. "In terms of the paperwork, he owns three-quarters and I own one-quarter," Gregg says. "All four of us are on the mortgage. We felt that we're a family; we'll take a chance together."

To save money, the Mitchells decided to oversee the renovation themselves with the help of a friend, Tyler Hays, who owns the furniture company BDDW. Hays, who had some experience as a contractor, supplied advice and workers to get the job done. They worked without plans or architectural drawings, sketching out their designs as they went. Although the couples at first planned to share a kitchen, Gregg says they eventually realized that they wanted to be "neighbors, not roommates." His ground-floor apartment has a separate street entrance. An ingenious layout made

OPPOSITE: The two families gather frequently in this light-filled den on the third floor. Beside the carved mahogany mantel, a flat-screen television hangs on the wall. The leather chair is by Finn Juhl, and the overhead light fixture is by David Weeks. ABOVE: The room's modern bookcase is by BDDW.

way for a sprawling front bedroom with a claw-foot tub, a living room, home office for Andrea, bathroom, and a galley kitchen. The refrigerator and the bathroom shower share a wall, or as Gregg puts it, yin-yang each other. "It's like a perfect ship," says their sister-in-law Pilar. "They use every inch."

Upstairs, the door is always unlocked to Chris and Pilar's triplex apartment. The kitchen, which also has a large walnut island, is the busiest room in the house. The room's fireplace, converted to gas to make sleepy mornings easier and more pleasant, is the heart of a small living area. It sits below an oil painting of a stern patriarch (it's actually a flea market find) and is flanked by two inviting antique Scottish armchairs.

The couple collects Danish modern furniture, which appears throughout the house, from the Arne Vodder rosewood credenza in the main-floor living room to the Peter Hvidt and Orla Molgaard-Nielson cabinet in the family room upstairs. The latter is the only room with a television. Its plaster walls, like most of those in the house, were taken apart and rewired to accommodate a state-of-the-art sound system.

ABOVE LEFT: A worn staircase leads from the triplex upstairs to the garden-level apartment downstairs owned by Gregg Mitchell and Andrea Chu. The antique spindle chairs are Swedish. ABOVE RIGHT: In the living room, a 1950s sofa is upholstered in a pattern adapted from an eighteenth-century Italian damask by Bennison Fabrics. OPPOSITE: A guest bedroom upstairs gets frequent use from visiting grandparents. The drawing over the fireplace is by Los Angeles artist Christina Hale.

On the top floor, in addition to two children's bedrooms (Henry was quickly joined by a younger brother, Willem) is a master bedroom that feels like a fancy hotel suite, with a large walk-in closet and a Carrara-walled bathroom that took the place of what was formerly a pass-through kitchen.

Those luxurious amenities are today's equivalent of the ornate plaster and inlaid parquet floors that the Victorians considered the sine qua non of high-end style. But, fortunately, here one doesn't come at the expense of the other. "It kills me when people take out the detail, but it's equally strange when I see people living in Victorian museums," Chris says. "In our neighborhood, the most successful renovations respect the history but embrace the way people live today."

RESTORATION NOTES WOODWORK

Those lucky enough to find antique woodwork intact in their town houses face a number of stewardship questions, from how to live with dark paneling in an already dark town house, to whether to strip the wood of its many layers of paint. If your home was built more than one hundred years ago, the woodwork is likely to have been made with old-growth wood whose lumber is prized today for its rich patina and durability.

HISTORY

Wood molding began as a practical solution as much as an ornamental one. Baseboards protected walls from water damage during floor mopping. Wainscoting shielded walls against damage by chair backs and saved energy by keeping homes weathertight. The earliest houses in North America had wood molding made on-site with hand planes and chisels. In the mid-nineteenth century, woodwork began to be machine made, which resulted in correspondingly lower prices. By the 1890s, builders of "spec" town houses could order such features as oak pier mirrors and mahogany balusters from millwork catalogs featuring pages of architectural elements and trimwork. The finest hardwood—mahogany, cherry, oak, and walnut—with the most intricate detailing was used most lavishly in the public areas on the parlor floor. The higher the floor, the less costly the wood—the master bedroom might feature poplar, for example, and the servants' floor at the top was often in pine.

WHAT TO LOOK FOR

Pier mirrors with columns and framing, pocket doors, ornate casing around doors, windows with pocket shutters, fireplace mantels and overmantels, built-in cabinetry, fretwork, paneling, and wainscoting.

WHEN TO STRIP

Many homeowners think they need to strip all antique woodwork down to the bare wood. But not all woodwork was meant to be what restorers call "wood finished." In pre-1840 homes, most wood was soft—usually pine—and painted. Later, builders gave homeowners the option of painted or finished wood. If lesser woods were used, they were hidden behind faux wood graining, paint, or colored varnishes. On the other hand, some hardwoods, such as mahogany and walnut, were meant to be gloriously on view and deserve to be stripped and fully restored. Start by carefully examining the woodwork. If painted, look for chips that allow you to see beneath the surface. If you can spot varnish or shellac under the chips, the woodwork was probably originally finished. A wood restorer should do small test scrapes to see what is underneath. This is how you will know if the cabinetry over the fireplace is walnut burl and worthy of restoration, or a soft wood and therefore fine to repaint.

REFINISHING WOODWORK

If you decide to strip, ask if the restorer uses a wet chemical method of paint stripping. The alternative, dry scraping, or sanding, can create a lot of lead dust. Another method using heat guns will vaporize the paint and can also release lead into the air. Once the wood is stripped, it will be sanded, patched, and filled. The last step is the finish, which is usually done with a varnish or shellac that requires no maintenance, or an unpigmented oil, which has a soft luster but must be redone every couple of years. If you plan to stain or paint the wood, insist on seeing samples on your own woodwork first, since color can look very different on varying types of wood.

THE FINAL FINISH

If the woodwork is in relatively good condition, you want just to refurbish the wood. This eliminates the stripping step and involves a thorough cleaning of the finish, which can make a huge aesthetic difference. For a linseed or tung oil finish, rub with lemon oil polish, which will lift some of the grime. To clean waxed wood, use a commercial wax stripper, a mild solution of white vinegar and water, or lemon oil polish, and then reapply a new wax topcoat. Both polyurethane and varnish finishes create a hard, waterproof coating that is very durable; to clean, wipe with a damp cloth.

SKYLINE VIEW

|BROOKLYN HEIGHTS, BROOKLYN|

Date built: Before 1840 | Width: 25 feet | Stories: 5 | Square footage: 8,000 | Bedrooms: 5 | Fireplaces: 6
Year purchased: 2006 | Length of renovation: 2½ years | House style: Greek Revival

This Greek Revival town house has a sober facade of plain brick. Step inside the house, and its patrician exterior turns into a five-floor mansion, exuberantly decorated and lavishly large. If that weren't enough, the view out the back is of New York's East River and, beyond it, the Manhattan skyline.

The story of this spacious brownstone is in many ways the tale of its Brooklyn Heights neighborhood, considered the first American suburb. When steam ferry service was established between Brooklyn and Manhattan in 1830, creating a quick twenty-minute commute, developers began to erect rows of houses on lots on the Brooklyn side of the waterfront, which had previously been country estates. Columbia Heights, the closest to the water,

PREVIOUS SPREAD, LEFT: The entry hall has a large canvas by the Israeli artist Tal R. The oak banister and staircase newels, all original to the house, were "taken apart and put back together," says architect Benjamin Baxt.
ABOVE: An informal dining area near the kitchen overlooks the rear deck, with its city view. RIGHT: The kitchen island has a curved Carrara marble top. OPPOSITE: The mantel displays the owner's collection of Mexican ceramics. Above it hangs a self-portrait by Jean Michel Basquiat.

"was always the street favored by the oligarchs," says Alex Herrera, director of technical services for the New York Landmarks Conservancy. "The fronts of these houses had New England reserve and gravitas. But the interiors were sumptuous."

By 1910, subways arrived in Brooklyn Heights, and the neighborhood began a long decline. The wealthy were the first to leave, and their costly homes, previously maintained by teams of servants, were often razed or turned into boardinghouses. Yet this one, which was built sometime before 1840, had somehow escaped that fate and has remained a single-family residence for most of its existence. One owner, from 1957 to 1995, was Donald F. Othmer, a chemist and inventor of the Xerox copier technology. In 1999, it was purchased by a couple who undertook an extensive renovation. They brought in Benjamin Baxt, a Manhattan-based architect and Brooklyn resident known for his expertise in restoring brownstones, to bring the house up-to-date in a neighborhood that by then had strict rules on historic property renovations.

For Baxt, the renovation became a balancing act between satisfying the clients' desire to maximize their million-dollar view and his own wish to visually connect the rear of the house with its two sister row houses. By studying the neighboring houses

PREVIOUS SPREAD, LEFT: The dining room has a dramatic scheme of hot pink flocked draperies, yellow upholstered Louis XV–style chairs, and an iron-and-Swarovski crystal chandelier from Hudson Furniture. The painting (left) is *Marrakesh* by Santi Moix. RIGHT: A painting by Norbert Schwontkowski hangs above an antique French sideboard.
OPPOSITE: The homeowners, avid collectors of contemporary art, turned a wall into a gallery. On display are pieces by Elliott Puckette, Daniel Richter, Henri Matisse, and a work titled "Pigcasso," painted by their son at the age of nine.

and looking at old photographs, he realized that the three homes once were linked by a series of canopied porches and wonderful undulating ironwork. "We told the clients we would get them the glass for those views, but that they would need to trade that with the landmarks commission for something," he says. "There was an awful extension on the back. We said let's get rid of it and re-create the remnants of the wonderful veranda that unified all three houses."

Baxt did a meticulous renovation in front of the house as well, where the bricks were cleaned down to the original clay and each mortar joint was carefully raked open and repointed with a special recipe. The brownstone details, including Corinthian-style pilasters and entablatures around the doorway, were redone by hand in cement plaster. Inside, the original oak staircase, which had rotted in sections, was taken

OPPOSITE: The master bedroom's turquoise was inspired by the view of sky outside its windows. THIS PAGE: The bedroom's walk-in closet accommodates a sofette (upper left) and a small desk (lower right). The bedroom furnishings include an Anglo-Indian ebony bookshelf (lower left), a Colonial-style bed, and a chair whose velvet upholstery matches the decor (upper right).

apart and put back together. But when the clients decided to remove the decorative plasterwork from the interior rooms rather than restore it, Baxt withdrew from the project. "I just couldn't do it with any conviction," he says.

Seven years later, the house was sold for that record price to an investment banker and his wife, a family with four young children. The sellers had decorated the house with antiques and formal furniture in a cream and beige palette. The new owners, who collect contemporary art, wanted the exact opposite: a family home with lots of color. "The wife told me, 'I cannot live with beige,'" says Ellen Hamilton, their interior designer.

The color jolt starts on the ground floor, where the hall and stairwell have been painted a dark saturated red, and continues upstairs, where the palette goes from turquoise to apple green to sherbet. "Red can be surprisingly neutral," says Hamilton, noting that the paint she used in the hallway, Picture Gallery Red (made by the British company Farrow & Ball), is particularly well suited to displaying artwork. The kitchen, with a view straight to the water, is chartreuse with a green-and-white Moroccan tile backsplash and a Carrara marble Eero Saarinen dining table.

ABOVE: The daughter's room, painted Pantone Orange Ochre, has an Anglo-Indian teak bed and hand-blocked Indian bedding. The artwork is by Donald Baechler. OPPOSITE: An upstairs library has green corduroy walls to match the sofa and a hot pink chandelier. The curtains are in a fabric by Designers Guild.

Baxt says the previous owners elected to maintain the formality of the parlor level. Today, this grand floor, though less stiff, remains a showpiece. The living room is filled with comfortable furnishings and a vibrant mix of ethnic patterns, from the contemporary take on a Suzani print that covers the ample chairs, to throw pillows in antique textiles, including Indian sari fabric and batik. Hervé Van der Straeten's bronze branch mirror hangs over the mantel. Another focal point of the room is a computerized artwork of a figure continuously walking by the artist Julian Opie.

And then there is that cinematic skyline view, now framed by zebra-print curtains. All in all, it's an exuberant display, and all the more surprising because it lies beyond this home's poker-faced front door.

OPPOSITE: The rear terrace has a panoramic view of the Manhattan skyline. The outdoor sofas are by John Hutton for Sutherland. **ABOVE:** Baxt removed an extension in back of the house and re-created the veranda and ironwork that had originally unified the home with its two neighbors. **LEFT:** The kitchen opens to an outdoor deck where the family dines in warm weather. A spiral iron stair leads to a balcony upstairs.

Modern Reinventions

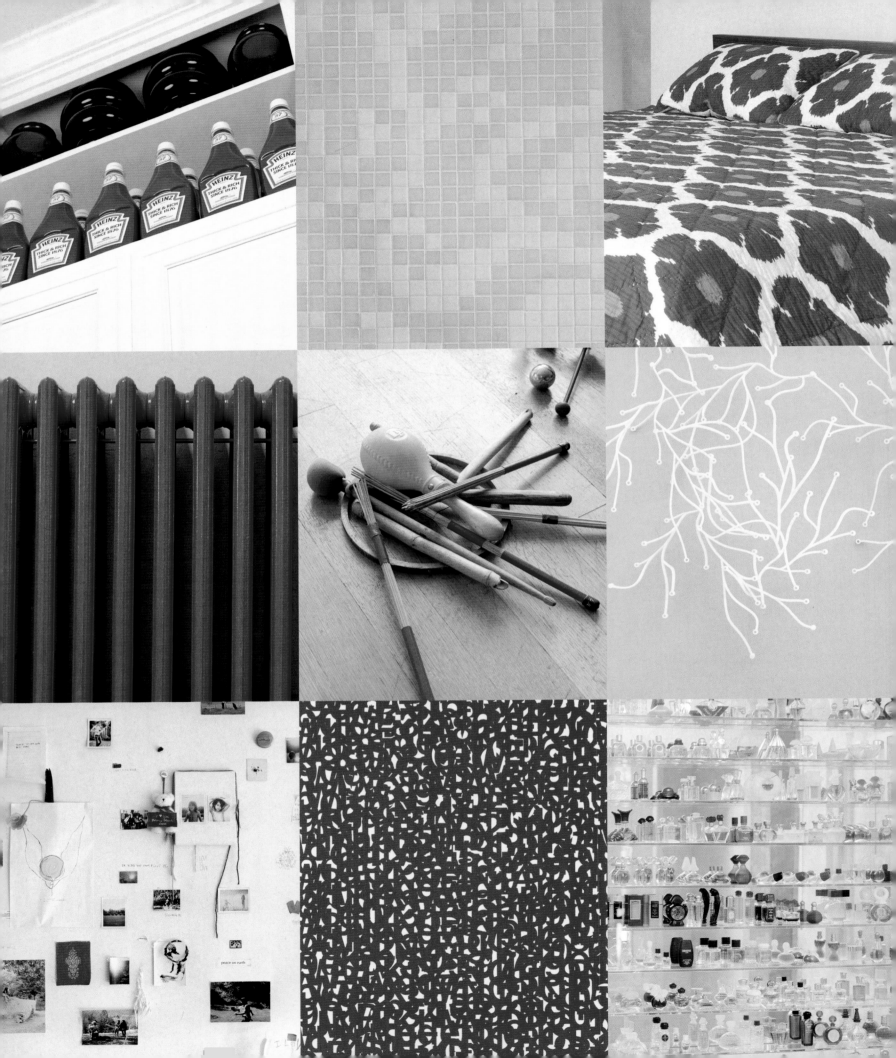

THE FACADES OF THE classic town houses on the following pages—whether brick, brownstone, or wood—look much as they did in the era they were built. Step across the threshold, however, and you travel through time from the eighteenth and nineteenth centuries and into the twenty-first. In Philadelphia's Society Hill, for example, a 1763 row house undergoes a surprising metamorphosis overseen by a team of modernist designers who are determined to push boundaries while preserving the past. In an 1880s town house in Baltimore, two graphic designers devise a clever scheme to bring more sunlight into its windowless heart, defying the interior's typically long and narrow layout.

Some of these historic houses are perfectly preserved from the street's-eye view, but on the inside reveal something else entirely. The sad fact is that not all town houses have survived the years with their interiors intact. In many cases their hand-made features—from ornamental entryways to decorative plaster and woodwork—have been lost to time, negligence, or lack of money for maintenance. Others are in even worse shape, their roofs caved in, their interiors in ruins. Thus, a homeowner may have no choice but to begin again. As two such projects featured here show, both marvels of glass and light, the best of these gut renovations combine the layout and flow of the classic row house with a thoroughly modern spirit.

MINIMALONIALISM

|SOCIETY HILL, PHILADELPHIA|

Date built: 1763 | Width: 20 feet | Stories: 5 | Square footage: 3,300 | Bedrooms: 4 | Fireplaces: 5
Year purchased: 2006 | Length of renovation: 9 months | House style: Colonial

In 1999, Minima, a glossy white showroom devoted to contemporary furniture, opened in Philadelphia's Old City. This historic neighborhood was emerging from a long period of neglect and becoming an exciting enclave of contemporary art galleries and restaurants. A new generation of homeowners was in turn moving into the nearby row houses of Society Hill, many of which date back to the eighteenth century. Though they would ogle the cutting-edge furnishings at Minima by designers such as Piero Lissoni and Jasper Morrison, many homeowners usually concluded that this furniture was too modern for a colonial home.

Minima's owner, Eugenie Perret, was frustrated. In Europe, where she had spent a lot of time, "people are open to mixing old and new," she says. She and her partner, industrial

OPPOSITE: In the living room an early mantel is in locally quarried King of Prussia black marble.
ABOVE: The reconstructed six-paneled front door is painted brick red and has an arched fanlight.
RIGHT: The entry vestibule leads into the parlor, and up two steps, into a dining room illuminated with a skylight.

designer Michael Schmick, set out to prove to Philadelphians that modernism and colonialism were not antithetical. Their 2005 show, Minimalonialism, cleverly juxtaposed the two styles.

One of the fans of the show was Andrew Hohns, a young investment banker and former Philadelphia mayoral candidate. Hohns had lived nearby on Elfreth's Alley, the last intact eighteenth-century American residential streetscape, with thirty-two row houses built between 1728 and 1836. To him, the Minima show proved that an old house didn't have to be old-fashioned. Two years later, he and his fiancée, Leah Popowich, bought a three-bay 1763 Colonial row house on Spruce Street in adjacent Society Hill. They approached Perret and Schmick to oversee the renovation and interior design. The Minima team was eager to put their theories into practice. "It was exactly the kind of house we were thinking about when we did our show," Perret says. "It had the old original floors, the shutters and plaster walls. We walked in and knew what needed to be done."

The house came with an invaluable resource—a lengthy thesis written about it by a student in the historic preservation program at the University of Pennsylvania. The research, which traces the property back to the original land grant from William

OPPOSITE: The parlor's minimalist aesthetic includes a sectional sofa by the Italian designer Piero Lissoni. ABOVE: In the dining room, Maarten Baas's Smoke dining chairs are emblematic of the "minimalonialist" approach, a design philosophy that fuses antique and modern styles.

Penn, recounts the history of the house from its first owner, the ship captain James Gibbon, to the 1960s resident who let it deteriorate so badly it was seized by the local redevelopment authority.

From the report, the owners learned how it had been altered over the years. The house was rehabilitated in the 1960s along with many of its Society Hill neighbors. The eighteenth-century brickwork, laid in a style called Flemish bond, was rebuilt around the entrance. The six-panel door, featuring a dramatic arched fanlight and reeded pilasters, was replaced. Inside, the house had survived two renovations—one in the nineteenth century, the second in the 1960s. Still, the house had many original features, including the frame and the staircase leading from the third floor to the attic. The wide pine floorboards had been cut from first-growth forests, where trees were often centuries old, yielding wood that is prized today for its lovely grain and dense ring count that makes it especially durable.

Schmick oversaw the renovation of the house, a process that over time became more complicated. He discovered that at some point—he suspects the 1960s—workers cut through the support beams that held up the second floor of the house. New structural I beams had to be installed in the living-room ceiling so that the house wouldn't collapse. Built without plumbing or electricity, the house had a web of pipes and

ABOVE: The multipaned bay window was added in the 1960s when the house was rehabilitated, along with many of its Society Hill neighbors. OPPOSITE: A lipstick-red Verner Panton chair adds a pop of color to the otherwise all-white kitchen.
FOLLOWING SPREAD, LEFT: Philippe Starck's translucent Eros chair is nestled in one of the attic's cozy nooks. RIGHT: A former bedroom was transformed into a spacious master bathroom covered in glass mosaic tile laid in a pattern resembling damask. Rather than remove the room's marble mantel, the fireplace was sealed and the mantel integrated into the room's design.

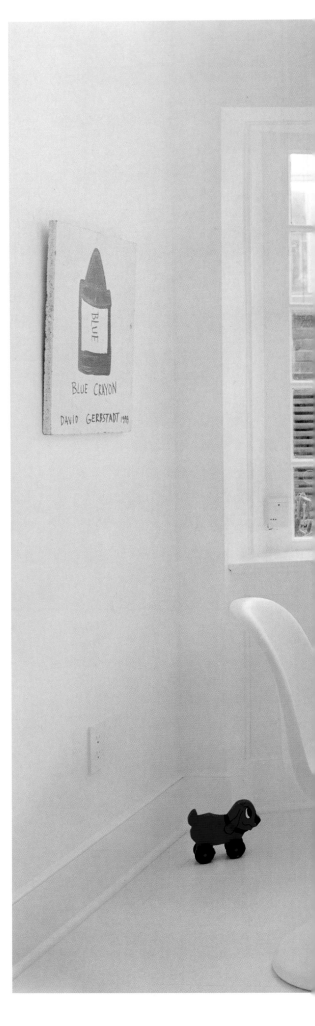

ABOVE: The master bedroom has a Baroque-inspired bed and an original fireplace. OPPOSITE: The fourth-floor attic, with its original beamed ceiling, now serves as a library and game room.

wires that needed to be updated. "By the end, we had touched every surface of the house," Schmick says.

The mandate was to carefully balance the old and the new. In the master bedroom, the antique shutters were moved forward a few inches so that modern fiberglass shades could be fitted inside the windows for an extra filter of light. The wood-beamed attic now serves as a modern library. Perret furnished the house with contemporary pieces—like those in the Minimalonialism show—that clearly referenced the past. In the dining room, for instance, a sleek black glass table is surrounded by a set of black baroque-looking chairs. In fact, they were created in 2006 by the Dutch designer Maarten Baas, who finishes his pieces by partially destroying them with fire.

For Hohns, quirky touches like the mantel in the bathroom, and the floors that still list up to six inches in places, make life interesting. Those are the details worth preserving in a house now in the third century of its existence. "A hundred years from now, none of the changes we are making will still be here but hopefully the original details will," he says. "In the end, you're just a steward of the house."

GRAPHIC POP

|BOLTON HILL, BALTIMORE|

Date built: Circa 1880 | Width: 18 feet | Stories: 4 | Square footage: 3,000 | Bedrooms: 4 | Fireplaces: 4
Year purchased: 1997 | Length of renovation: 12 months | House style: Italianate

Walking through Bolton Hill, with its rows of austere town houses set back from the sidewalks, one can easily lose oneself in the past. Built in the nineteenth century, the Baltimore neighborhood attracts history lovers and preservationists. But behind the walls of one stately row house is the home of a couple that is as passionate about modernism as they are about Victorian architecture. Ellen Lupton and J. Abbott Miller are both stars of the graphic design world. He is a partner at the international design firm Pentagram, while she is a contemporary design curator at the Cooper-Hewitt National Design Museum, and a director of the graphic design MFA program at the Maryland Institute College of Art.

They met and married in 1991 in New York, but with two young children, Jay and Ruby, they quickly found the city crowded. In 1997, they moved back to Lupton's native Baltimore, trading a tiny Manhattan apartment for a classic Baltimore Victorian in the heart of Bolton Hill, an intact late nineteenth-century neighborhood of town houses, churches, parks, and fountains. "I knew Bolton Hill as a child and had always lusted after it as a more luxurious version of where I had lived," Lupton says.

It was an unconventional move for the jet-setting couple, especially since Miller would now be commuting to New York, spending two days a week working at his Manhattan office, and the rest of the time telecommuting from a vintage storefront he rented across the street from their new home. They also had to reconcile their cutting-edge tastes with their traditional surroundings. To Miller and Lupton, it wasn't such a stretch: the classic town house's tall ceilings and boxy volumes were reminiscent in scale of a modern loft. The key was to brighten the decor and make the most of the light that flows through the space.

It helped that Lupton's father, William, is an experienced Baltimore contractor. Working without plans or drawings, he and Miller took on an extensive renovation of

the house. "We didn't know what we would discover as we ripped walls apart," Miller says. "It was a very organic and fun way to work."

One discovery was that the house originally had two skylights that had once illuminated two separate stairwells—the public staircase and the servants' stairs. Like so many other Baltimore town houses, this one had been partitioned for years into apartments. The servants' stairs had been removed and that skylight covered up. Miller and his father-in-law uncovered this second skylight and came up with an ingenious plan to channel the light downward. On the top floor, a light well reflects through a glass-walled shower to an atrium in the master bathroom on the floor below.

The restoration of the house, under the watchful eye of the local preservation association, was in many ways by the book. Windowframes were replaced with new wooden ones that reproduced the decorative flourishes of the originals. Old pine floors were restored. The landscaping plan for the tiny front yard was dutifully submitted for approval. Yet Lupton and Miller's love of design and bold color is everywhere, from the vibrant blue of the front door to the orange kitchen, whose color was inspired by the label of Veuve Clicquot champagne. The decor mixes antique Oriental rugs with modern posters, including several designed by Miller, and the couple's collection of furniture and textiles by a who's who of modern and contemporary designers, including Jean Prouvé, Florence Knoll, and Hella Jongerius. Meanwhile, all the radiators in the house were stripped and repainted in shiny red automotive paint by a local firm, Baltimore Finishing Works. "It was such a hassle to have it done, we thought: Why not make them remarkable and special?" Lupton says.

Modernists that they are, Lupton and Miller couldn't resist a more radical departure in the back of the house, where the zoning rules tend to be looser. At the end of their long and narrow garden, they built a glass-and-steel carport with a cantilevered roof that would not look out of place in Venice Beach. Designed by Baltimore architect Doug Bothner of Ziger/Snead Architecture, the garage has transparent doors on two sides, encasing the family's navy blue MINI Cooper in glass, like a specimen in a museum exhibit. When the family entertains, they pull their car onto the street and roll up the glass door facing the garden for an extra party space. "It's as close to a California modern sensibility," Miller says, "as we could manage in Bolton Hill."

OPPOSITE: The couple collects mid-twentieth-century modern furniture, like the rear parlor's Florence Knoll sofa. TOP: A sunny bay leads out onto a porch set up for outdoor dining. ABOVE: The room's keystone mantel. TOP RIGHT: The artwork over the sofa includes a poster by the Swiss graphic designer Cornell Windlin and another, designed by Miller, on Henri de Toulouse-Lautrec. BOTTOM RIGHT: A vintage cabinet by Paul McCobb holds an all-white dinner service.

PREVIOUS SPREAD, LEFT: Homeowner Abbott Miller's Merge wallcovering, for KnollTextiles, made from overlapping lines of the font Helvetica, is in the permanent collection at the Cooper-Hewitt National Design Museum. In his town house, the design appears in black in the sitting room off the master bedroom, accompanied by a silhouette print by artist Kara Walker and a Jasper Morrison Glo-Ball lamp for Flos. RIGHT: The same wallpaper pattern in red in a powder room downstairs.
OPPOSITE: A third-floor bathroom—formerly a warren of small closets—has gray subway tile and a walk-in shower with frosted-glass walls illuminated by a skylight. ABOVE LEFT: The master bathroom is in a dark salmon red, a shade favored by the architect Le Corbusier. LEFT: In the master bedroom, above an original mantel, a poster for the 1960s film *Blow-Up* matches the room's hot pink Verner Panton chair.

RESTORATION NOTES COLOR

Classic town houses often have central rooms without a single window, enormous stair halls, and fourteen-foot ceilings with more icing than a wedding cake, all of which require a well-thought-out color strategy.

HISTORY

In the past, the decorating style of the day would have dictated your color choices. A Federal town house would have been painted in such vibrant shades as powder blue, mint, rose, pumpkin, and mustard, set off by cream woodwork and polished wood floors. A Greek Revival town house had a more subdued palette of putty white with forest green and silver gray. And an Italianate brownstone might have been furnished in turquoise, claret, plum, and every shade of brown.

THE STAIR HALL Eve Ashcraft, an architectural color consultant in New York, chooses a single palette to give the stair hall uniformity as it winds its way from the bottom to the top floor. However, because so much of one color can look overwhelming, she'll tone it down by decorating the walls with art or photography in coordinating frames. Another approach is to apply paneling to the bottom half of the stair hall.

BRIGHT CHOICES Light, or the lack of it, is often a deciding factor in selecting a town house's color palette—especially in middle rooms without windows or halls and stairs absent skylights. Any dark space can be brightened with good lighting, but paint can also go a long way toward lightening a space. Look for shades with a reflectance value (LRV) of at least 70 percent. Still, not every space in a town house needs to feel sunlit. Built before the invention of such amenities as air-conditioning and ultraviolet-filtered glass, town houses were equipped with shutters and draperies that were drawn

to moderate temperature and protect fabrics and furniture from fading in the sunlight. Darker hues such as dramatic reds and chocolate browns can be wonderfully atmospheric in an old town house.

ROOM TO EXPERIMENT Town houses have many self-contained areas such as the front entry hall or upper bedrooms, which lend themselves to color experimentation. "You can have a blue room next to a green room next to a red one," says Ashcraft, who adds that "the architecture supports the shift more than in other house forms."

PARLOR GAMES For rooms as dramatic as the high-ceilinged double parlor, the color scheme will be guided by such factors as the furnishings, artwork, and architectural flourishes (mantels, mirrors, and chandeliers). The front parlor, typically the room with better light conditions, can handle a bold hue. Given the scale, however, it's best to mitigate a large expanse of strong color with curtains and art that can be stacked vertically on a

wall. To accentuate the room's details, divide the parlor's ample crown moldings into three sections and vary tones of whites and grays to enhance shadows. Consider painting parlor ceilings a pale warm gray, rather than the typical white, since the darker shade makes the large rooms feel more intimate.

CHOOSING HUES Several paint firms offer researched palettes based on period architecture. Other companies offer more contemporary color schemes and broader selections of whites and neutrals. Since lighting conditions can vary from town house to town house, or even in a single room at different times of day, avoid choosing a color based only on the hue of a paint chip. Instead, narrow your color selections and buy sample color pots of paint in several shades in the same family, as well as intensities of a single hue. The best way to test a color is to paint a swatch on a wall and observe how the shade changes on sunny versus cloudy days, or from morning to evening.

EXTERIORS Unless you are dealing with a Queen Anne Victorian in San Francisco, where the color choices are practically infinite, there will be limited opportunities for color expression on the exterior of your town house. But even brick and brownstone can be a color statement, with masonry ranging from gray to orange and brownstone from rust to deep chocolate brown.

FITTING IN For a town house, especially one that is part of a row, one consideration is how the facade will blend with its surroundings. Ashcraft recommends getting what she calls the "gestalt" of a block. Note the color schemes of neighboring homes. For historic houses, most people pick a traditional exterior palette that will harmonize with its neighbors. Local historic preservation agencies and libraries can provide images of how any style of town house would have originally looked.

DO SWATCHES One consideration is your house's position in relation to the sun.

A facade that appears bright white in a home with a southern exposure could read as yellow in one facing north. Thus, even on the outside of your home, it is always worthwhile to use color swatches. Exterior accessories—from window frames to door surrounds and shutters—also dictate color choice. These will generally match, with all the details in glossy black, for instance, or linen white.

FRONT DOORS Where there is possibility for individuality, take advantage. In most brick or brownstone homes, the front door presents one such opportunity, and most landmarked neighborhoods will have rules on permissible door colors. Fine Paints of Europe (see Where to Find It, page 270), which sells top-of-the-line exterior enamel paints, has a color chart based on the colors of doors in Holland, with shades ranging from Tulip Red to Delft Blue. Their Web site also offers free instructions on how to paint a front door, from sanding, priming, and brushwork, to achieving that gleaming, flawless finish that makes for an impressive entrance.

LIGHT BOX

Date built: 1840 | Width: 25 feet | Stories: 5 | Square footage: 3,900 | Bedrooms: 4 | Fireplaces: 2
Year purchased: 2001 | Length of renovation: 2 years | House style: Greek Revival

One morning Mark Borthwick bicycled to the farmers' market at the foot of the Brooklyn Bridge. He was letting his inspiration guide him as he planned the menu for a party to be held at his town house that night. "Did you get my e-mail? Are you coming?" asked Borthwick, a fashion photographer who had woken up that morning and decided to invite more than a hundred of his closest friends to dinner. His wife, the fashion designer Maria Cornejo, was in Paris for fashion week, and this inveterate party-thrower was feeling sociable.

The evening was magical. Adults and children mingled in the kitchen as Borthwick, an excellent cook, prepared ripe tomato and basil bruschetta and lamb burgers wrapped

TOP: In a ground-flour den, artwork and personal photos are casually tacked to the wall. ABOVE: A console in the entry hall is arranged with mementos. OPPOSITE: The staircase was designed with open risers to allow light to pass through the house.

in beet leaves. The garden was lit with tiki torches, and wine was poured. From the outside, looking through the rear glass wall into the interior, the home looked like a doll house glowing with light.

Not every old house can be brought back to life in its entirety. That was certainly the case with this 1840 Greek Revival row house in Cobble Hill, one of Brooklyn's prettiest neighborhoods. The home had been abandoned and occupied by squatters for more than a decade. At one point a plumbing explosion had left an eighteen-foot crater in the middle of the house. "There was mold everywhere," Borthwick recalls. "It was very unhealthy and dangerous, and the house had been taken over by cats."

Today, this formerly squalid building has been elegantly renovated by Manhattan architects Fernlund + Logan in a design that perfectly fuses both historic and modern concepts of town house living. Beneath the improvisational decor is a house where every detail has been carefully considered, even if the decision was made to err on the side of simplicity. "We didn't want a house that looked too designed," Cornejo says. "We just wanted a great space where we could live our life."

Borthwick and Cornejo had always dreamed of building a house. They were living in Manhattan when they went to look at the brick town house, which was on

Amity Street, in Brooklyn. Borthwick tells the story this way: "It was a mighty fine evening, and when we saw the sign for Amity Street we smiled and said, 'Wouldn't it be nice to live on a street called Amity?'" The fact that the house was in irredeemable condition on the inside didn't bother them, Cornejo says, since they "didn't want to tear something down with historical value."

One of the first calls they made was to architect Neil Logan, whose sister they knew when they lived in Paris. Borthwick showed Logan a photograph of an architect's studio in Paris that was located in an old factory building. He liked its transparency and the fact that the industrial architecture wasn't trying too hard. Logan proposed to restore the facade of the building while creating entirely new architecture within— an airy and light-filled house where almost nothing is hidden from view.

The building came with a sagging, two-story green clapboard addition in the rear. Logan and his partner and wife, Solveig Fernlund, proposed tearing it down and building a new three-floor extension. The back wall was to be built entirely out of industrial putty-glazed factory windows. But when the plans were submitted to the neighborhood landmarks review board, they faced serious opposition. Many of their neighbors objected to the new glass rear facade and worried that it would end up looking like a Madison Avenue storefront. A compromise was finally reached to reduce the extension to two floors and to configure the industrial windows as four-paned casement windows so they would better resemble others in the neighborhood.

In a classic town house, the main entryway opens onto the parlor level and a solid staircase leading up. In this case, the architects deliberately reversed this arrangement, so that the main entryway opens onto a slim staircase immediately

OPPOSITE: On the ground floor, the putty-glazed windows open on to the back garden (top). The home's decor, like this sheepskin-draped chair (bottom right) and, everywhere, a profusion of houseplants (bottom left), has a bohemian feel. ABOVE: The kitchen's birch plywood wall credenza has a Corian countertop.

PREVIOUS SPREAD, LEFT: In the living room, a walnut sideboard by Philip Mainzer for the German company e15 sits below a drawing by the artist Rita Ackermann. RIGHT: Borthwick's art and photography studio is located on the top floor of the house, which has a large skylight. OPPOSITE: The rear wall of the two-story addition was built of welded steel plates and factory windows (made by Bliss Nor-Am) that are hinged and open outward from the top. In the living room, the furniture is often pushed to the corners to make way for all-night jam sessions led by Borthwick, whose musical alter ego is Will Shine.

pointing downward to the kitchen and garden on the level below. Like everything else in the house, the design of the stairs—wooden slats that float over nonexistent risers—is as unobtrusive as possible. The view is virtually unobstructed to the home's glass rear wall. "We were trying to create a seamlessness between the addition and the rest of the house," Logan says.

Since he loves to cook, Borthwick considered installing a restaurant-style kitchen but decided it would look too heavy. Instead, the sink, appliances, and cabinetry were concealed in a pale wood wall credenza that looks more like a piece of furniture than a hardworking kitchen. The room is sparsely furnished, with two benches that frame a European oak table by the German company e15, for whom Borthwick has designed a line of furniture. Not wanting to clutter the space with radiators, they installed radiant heat in the floor. "It's the lightest kitchen possible," Logan says. "You barely notice it."

Also unusual is the layout of the bedroom floor, which was designed to radiate from the center hall like a pinwheel. Their son's bedroom opens onto a shared bathroom that in turn pivots into the master bedroom. Sliding panels take the place of doors: hidden inside the walls, the doors glide into position to create an almost seamless plane when privacy is desired. "It is the one floor that is frequented only by us," Borthwick says. His studio is one floor above the bedrooms, so the house is always filled with visitors.

The front of the town house reveals nothing of the transformation within. Maria's brother George Cornejo, who acted as the contractor on the project, restored the home's facade in the traditional manner. He replaced the damaged bricks and installed a new front door and period-style chain windows. The couple's money ran out before they could replace the front stoop, one of several projects they plan to do when their finances permit. "It's a work in progress," Maria says.

One winter weekend afternoon, she and her family were relaxing at home, seated on the living room floor, drinking Lapsang Souchong tea. Near the wall of windows, a citrus tree was dripping with oranges, and orchids were in bloom—the beneficiaries of a row house whose back wall is now drenched with sun. Cornejo says she would still like to properly furnish the living room, which is now filled with musical instruments and mismatched furniture draped in antique quilts. For the most part, however, her house is just as she had imagined it: a light-filled vessel where she and her husband and their two children can play and work and dream.

OPPOSITE: The bathroom, located in between the two bedrooms on the third floor, has a slatted wood floor in marine-grade cedar, and is equipped with radiant heat, as is the entire house. ABOVE RIGHT: The master bedroom, which has one of the home's two fireplaces, is sparsely furnished. "We want our house to be as un-designed as possible," Borthwick says. RIGHT: The son's bedroom has a loft bed and a hanging outdoor wicker chair from Ikea.

FOLLOWING SPREAD, LEFT: In good weather the family treats the garden as an extension of the house. RIGHT: From the back of the house, the new glass-and-steel extension has the feel of a bilevel conservatory.

BRICKS AND GLASS

|GREENWICH VILLAGE, NEW YORK CITY|

Date built: 1855 | Width: 24 feet | Stories: 5 | Square footage: 4,200 | Bedrooms: 4 | Fireplaces: 3
Year purchased: 2004 | Length of renovation: 2 years | House style: Greek Revival

The town house was part of a row of Greek Revival homes on a street paved with Belgian block, the nineteenth-century successor to the cobblestone. The location was perfect, but the real estate broker was discouraging. "You won't like it," she told Adam Gordon. From the front, the twenty-four-foot-wide house looked as if it needed work but could easily be restored. The back of the house, however, was completely walled in and surrounded by the thirty-five-foot-high walls of neighboring buildings.

Many prospective buyers would have moved on, but Gordon, a real estate developer, immediately recognized the home's uniqueness. To him, the walled garden was a rare asset, giving the house a sense of privacy in a dense urban landscape. "It's not like those

PREVIOUS SPREAD, LEFT: The second-floor living room overlooks the walled garden. ABOVE: The living room's serene modernist decor includes a Brazilian modernist chair and a custom wood coffee table. Artwork by Donald Baechler hangs over the fireplace. RIGHT: In the home office, a Damien Hirst spin painting hangs above a free-form wood slab table by Andrianna Shamaris. OPPOSITE: Architect Steven Harris re-created the back facade of the town house in walls of glass.

transparent buildings where everything is on display." By contrast, with this house, Gordon says, "No one knows it is here."

He bought the town house and hired Steven Harris, a Yale University architecture professor, to oversee the renovation. The result is starkly modern, though you wouldn't know it from the street. The architect restored the facade to perfection, replacing the front door with a historically correct one and re-creating its missing French balconies and decorative ironwork. But step inside, and the architecture is utterly transformed—five minimalist floors that now culminate in a back wall made almost entirely of glass. Best of all, Harris took the home's alleged liability—those three blind walls—and made it a virtue. The massive windows look directly onto the private garden, which is now an oasis of bamboo, water, and green lawn.

Before beginning the renovation, Harris hired a researcher to document the history of the town house, which had lived a long, hard life and had the scars to show for it. The home was built in 1855 by a house painter on land that was once submerged under the Hudson River. In later years, it became a boardinghouse for immigrants and tradesmen. There were twenty-nine people living in the house at one time during the Depression, and for decades the block, which was semi-industrial, was also home to a sausage factory and an all-night pigs' knuckles pickler. By the time Gordon bought it, the building was in such poor condition, and had been altered so many times, that Harris believed a gut renovation was the only solution.

"Even if you wanted to perfectly restore it," he says, "you would have had to demolish the interior and start over."

Rather than re-create the house as a period piece, Harris instead designed a new modernist interior influenced by two of his idols, Philip Johnson and Louis Kahn. The meticulously restored facade now fronts an airy interior, with all-white walls, pale floors, and windowpanes fourteen feet wide and seven inches thick, which were so big they had to be lifted over the garden walls by crane. Meanwhile, the backyard, once littered with trash and rusted lawn furniture, was transformed into a private oasis, with a reflecting pool and a back wall planted with thirty-four-foot bamboo stalks that Gordon procured on eBay.

The interiors may be restrained, but the finishes are luxurious. The living room floor, in white Imperial Danby marble from Vermont, is contiguous with the matching marble of the patio. The sumptuous marble bathroom's walls and floors are in tan Crema Marfil marble. Throughout the house, the architecture is subtly dazzling, especially on the penthouse floor, where Harris plays a visual trick. The penthouse consists of two terraces—one indoor, one outdoor—that perfectly mirror each other, right down to the matching fireplaces.

PREVIOUS SPREAD, LEFT: On the first floor, the dining room has a Brazilian rosewood table and vintage George Nakashima chairs. The artwork is a Louis Waldon silkscreen of Andy Warhol's *The Last Supper*. RIGHT: The adjacent living room, along with the entire ground level, has floors in Imperial Danby marble from the last active quarry in Vermont.
ABOVE: The kitchen has a marble-topped wooden island and cerused oak cabinetry.
OPPOSITE: The spectacular garden room, visible from every floor, has a reflecting pool with koi fish. The grass is Synlawn, a synthetic turf.

An unusual feature of the home is the perfectly mowed turf in the back garden—an illusion, as it turns out. It began as a seeded lawn, but when Gordon had trouble finding someone to keep it regularly mowed, he had the idea of replacing it with an artificial turf. The maintenance-free result—inspired by the landscaping of a Las Vegas hotel—looks almost real and stays green through all four seasons.

The town house's utterly transformed interiors might not please some preservationists, but the American Institute of Architects liked it well enough to give it an architectural honor award in 2007. For Gordon, the house retains the best features of the past while looking to the future. A longtime Buddhist, he takes a spiritual view of renovation, believing that a home—like any living being—can be reborn. "Houses that sustain themselves," says Gordon, "are the ones that reincarnate most successfully."

ABOVE: The luxurious master bathroom spans the entire width of the house. LEFT: Gordon's two young sons share a bedroom. OPPOSITE: A hallway leading to the master bathroom is lined with built-in closets in paneled lined oak. In the bedroom (bottom), concealed window shades, activated by remote control, provide privacy.

FOLLOWING SPREAD: The top floor consists of three spaces: an outdoor deck with a view of neighboring brownstones (above left); an outdoor terrace whose fireplace mirrors the one inside (bottom left); and an indoor room with furnishings by Andrianna Shamaris (right).

Buyer's and
Renovator's Guide

BEFORE YOU BUY

Restoring an old town house is undeniably romantic. But what are you really getting yourself into? While there is almost no restoration project that deep pockets and time and effort can't fix, here are some tips on how to know when a house is right for you—and when to walk away.

GO FOR IT WHEN

THE HOUSE SPEAKS TO YOU
This should be a prerequisite for buying any home, but particularly an antique that will require continual care and feeding. The work and investment will be worth it only if you are in love. If the house doesn't speak to you emotionally from the start, it never will.

IT PASSES INSPECTION
To obtain a thorough appraisal of the house's condition, hire a reliable house inspector. (Get referrals from local preservation agencies, architects, and neighbors.) Realtors are often ready to jump in with suggestions for inspectors, but such recommendations are best avoided as they can sometimes present a conflict of interest. Understand that the inspector is legally required to list absolutely every issue in a house or face a lawsuit. As a result, many real estate inspection reports can at first sound alarming. Buyers need to learn to filter out serious problems from fixable ones. Ask the inspector for a ballpark estimate on how much it will cost to correct any serious problems. If that figure is within your budget, proceed with the sale.

YOU'VE DONE YOUR RESEARCH
A surprising number of homeowners are so seduced by the charm of an old town house that they forget to do their homework. The house may speak to you, but soon enough, so will the leaky roof, or the neighborhood landmarks office regarding renovation permits. Before his clients buy a town house, Charleston restoration expert Richard Marks performs what he calls a "distortion survey," where he examines an old house for irregularities and advises on what it would take to fix any serious issues. When you are ready to buy, make sure you are getting a fair price by asking your real estate broker for recent "comps," or prices for sales of comparable buildings in the neighborhood. And don't assume you can extend your building's height or build an addition on the back without carefully checking with your local zoning office.

YOU HAVE A STRONG CONSTITUTION
Or you like surprises. "Anyone who renovates an old town house has to be a realist," says Nicholas Stern, vice president of Taconic Builders, a high-end Manhattan construction firm. "These buildings have gone through a historical evolution, usually starting as a single-family residence, then turned into tenements and chopped up into Swiss cheese. Then someone comes along and wants to turn it back into a single-family home. When you start to tinker, the force of time comes undone, and a lot of people aren't prepared for that." It's a safe assumption that pretty much everything—from the wiring to the roof—will need a substantial degree of work.

YOU ARE IN IT FOR THE LONG TERM
Leave house-flipping to the professionals. Most town house owners have at least a five-year horizon for owning their homes, which compensates for the time and expense you will need to put into it. The longer you live in your house, the more you spread out the costs of moving, buying, and renovating and the less you need to worry about the ups and downs of the housing market. And remember that the biggest return on your investment is the joy of living in a beautiful antique residence.

WALK AWAY IF

YOU ARE IN A HURRY
Restoring a house is labor intensive and can take many months. Every aspect requires research, from finding the right contractor and architect to deciding what to do with everything from the masonry to the windows. If you take the time to thoughtfully evaluate and execute these renovations (few of which come in on time or on budget), then they can last for many years; do them the wrong way and before you know it you will have to do them all over again.

THE HOUSE HAS TENANTS
One of the virtues of the town house model is that some floors can be converted into separate apartments, affording an income stream for the homeowner. The caveat for a town house buyer is that existing tenants often have rent-controlled or -stabilized apartments, and it can be extremely difficult to get them to leave. Clem Labine, founder of the *Old-House Journal*, cites an example of a friend who bought a Brooklyn row house in 1964. The last rent-controlled tenant moved out in 2003. "If you think of yourself as a nice person," he says, "you might not want to buy a house with tenants."

THE HOUSE IS BEING UNLOADED MIDRENOVATION
If a seller is bolting halfway into a town house renovation, buyer beware. It usually means there are serious issues with the house. These can range from discovering that past renovations violated local building codes or that structural problems are so severe that the entire home needs to be taken apart and put back together again.

A nineteenth-century brick hearth was one of the many original details still intact in a Savannah town house (see Ghost Story, page 147).

THE FLOOR IS SERIOUSLY UNEVEN

A little lean can be charming. But a deviation in the floor of more than one inch can sometimes be a signal that a house has serious structural concerns. The same goes for the main staircase: if one side of the steps is considerably higher than the other side, the house may be settling and could become unstable. The mortise-and-tenon construction of most old town houses is prone to structural problems, which can be hugely expensive to repair. Other signs of settling include buckling facades, cracks in tile floors, and cracking at the top of walls. But leave it to a professional house inspector to make the final diagnosis.

THE HOUSE HAS TERMITES

For some, termites are a deal breaker. Others are more tolerant. After more than a century, it's rare for a house made largely of wood never to have encountered some kind of wood-destroying insect. Leave them unchecked, however, and they can do serious damage. The telltale sign that termites are present is the hanging iciclelike structures that the insects build, often in the basement. If your inspector notices signs of termite treatment, ask the seller for a detailed report from the previous analysis and treatment. Then ask an exterminator to compare the previous report with current conditions. If you buy the house, try to leave a six-inch space around the perimeter of the basement clear of obstructions so that the wood can be regularly inspected for the presence of termites.

DETECTIVE WORK: RESEARCHING YOUR OLD HOUSE

If you have ever wondered who built your town house and when, or what it originally looked like, or who lived there before you did, try looking for the clues to its history. If your house is in a designated historical neighborhood, and you are planning any alterations to the exterior—from changing the windows to adding a porch—you will need to be armed with information about how your home looked when it was first built. Finally, before undertaking a renovation, it helps to learn as much as you can about your house's architecture and construction. Here are some research avenues to explore:

ORAL HISTORY

Living witnesses—previous owners, neighbors—can often provide a wealth of information about your building. They may have architectural plans, photographs of the house, old maps of the area, or personal records pertaining to the house. Talk to them about what they remember about the house. Can they recall if it was altered in any way? Who lived there? Was it damaged by any natural (or unnatural) incidents? What kind of lifestyle did the occupants lead? Don't overlook the telephone book as a way of tracking people down.

FINDING DOCUMENTS

Often you can find public records on your house that go back to the lot's original land deed. You can also research the chain of title (ownership) and occupancy, a useful tool for discovering all the major (and minor) characters who have played a role in your house's history. Researching a house is tricky, as there has never been a uniform method for compiling and maintaining this information. Some places to check include:

YOUR LOCAL LIBRARY

Reference archivists and librarians can steer you to the agencies that keep building records of your neighborhood. The library or a local historical society will also be a source for early neighborhood atlases, many of which indicate individual structures that existed on a lot in a given year. If an 1860 atlas showed an empty lot, and the 1870 atlas indicated a structure on that location, you know that a building was constructed there in the intervening years. You can also search a library's newspaper archives for references to builders, architects, and prior owners, once you obtain their names.

PUBLIC ARCHIVES

Building and tax departments, municipal archives, and historical societies keep a variety of records tracing both a property's history and a list of owners and occupants. Try to find *land deeds,* which record real and personal property transfers. If the deed is very old, be mindful that the current house might be a replacement for an earlier one. Keep track of the names listed on the deeds and look them up in *city directories,* early listings that included not only names and addresses but also occupations and spouse names. *Census records,* taken every ten years, list all the residents of a building. This information can be accessed through municipal archives or via the genealogical Web site ancestry.com. *State probate records* are a source for last wills and testaments, which can give a sense of household inventories such as furniture.

SANBORN FIRE MAPS

From 1867 to 1970, the Sanborn Map Company created fire insurance maps of more than twelve thousand American towns and cities. The maps, also called plat books, gave information on a building's footprint, size, shape, construction materials, height, location of windows and doors, and other details that were used to estimate fire risk. Now digitized, the maps are available by subscription and can be accessed at many libraries. In Savannah, for example, the maps were created in 1884, 1898, and 1916. "They're a little window into what was happening on your lot in each of those years," says Lucinda M. Spracher of Bricks and Bones Historical Research in Savannah, who helped trace the lineage on the Oliver town house (see Ghost Story, page 147). "Was there a carriage house in back? Were there waterlines? Each map is a snapshot of your home at a moment in history."

OLD PHOTOS

Former owners are a great source of images of what your house looked like in the past. Many cities and towns documented each building in their community in "tax photos." Some of these archives have been digitized and are available online. Other sources of old photos include libraries, historical societies, and colleges and universities. Don't overlook the attic, which can be an incredible repository of old photos, documents, and artifacts.

ARCHITECTURAL DRAWINGS

The original plans of a town house are invaluable, but they are one of the hardest documents to find. Sometimes you get lucky and find the plans among the seller's paperwork on the house. In most cases, they won't have them. If you know the name of the architect, find out if the practice still exists—they might have retained the records. An architecture firm may have donated their files to local libraries or historical societies. Check old newspapers—in the nineteenth century, builders sometimes published floor plans to advertise their new town house developments, much as they do today.

ON-SITE ARCHAEOLOGY

The history of an old house is often embedded in its structure. You just have to know where to look. Charleston restorer Richard Marks, who worked on the Horton house (see Charleston Revival, page 21) spends months studying an old town house before he begins a renovation. He counts the number of layers of paint on different sections of the home as a clue to its history. If one door has twenty layers of paint, and another has just five, the latter one was probably added at a later date. He inspects walls for "ghost marks," or faint lines where plaster cornices were likely removed. In the Horton house, he found a ghost mark on a brick wall, proof that an early staircase had been removed from that location. He can also perform what he calls a "nail typology," analyzing nails in the frames and floorboards to discover when they were assembled.

OR HIRE SOMEONE ELSE TO DO THE WORK

House researchers can be hired on an hourly or project basis to do the legwork for you. For referrals, ask your local historical society, or contact the Society of American Archivists in Chicago (see Where to Find It, page 270).

WORKING WITH ARCHITECTS AND CONTRACTORS

If you are planning any major work—from a kitchen to a facade restoration—you'll need to hire a contractor and possibly an architect. Here are some tips on hiring and working with architects and contractors:

LIVE THERE FIRST

If at all possible, live in your house for at least a few months before you begin your renovation. Julianne Moore didn't live in her house, but she and her family did rent another town house before moving into the one they bought and renovated, which she says was an invaluable experience. In the first house, the playroom was in the basement and the children's bedrooms were on the top floor.

The result was that her two young children's toys were scattered all over the house. When she renovated her brownstone, she put the playroom on the top floor and the children's rooms just one floor below. Once you spend time in your town house, you might also discover that some of the features you initially thought had to go—the ornate Victorian fretwork, or the dark woodwork—might start to grow on you.

SOMETIMES IT PAYS TO HIRE AN ARCHITECT

Given the expense, many renovators proceed without an architect and let their contractor oversee the design. But if you are doing any major work, with a budget of about $70,000 or above, hire an architect. A good one can actually save you money by finding contractors and workers through a competitive bid process. The architect's role can include preparing plans that show contractors and workers exactly what is required, managing the project, and filing plans with the city. "Not hiring an architect is like being your own attorney in court," says Alex Herrera of the New York Landmarks Conservancy. "You can do that to a certain extent, but having an architect takes away a lot of the stress."

GET REFERRALS

The expert you choose is the most important decision you will make, so don't shortchange your research. It makes sense to hire professionals who have worked in the neighborhood, since they will have experience with local architecture and building codes. But you need to do more than just ask friends and neighbors for referrals. According to *Consumer Reports*, 41 percent of readers who hired a contractor reported some problem with their project, including shoddy installation (13 percent), late starts (13.5 percent), sloppy workers (11 percent), and poor coordination (12 percent). Ask to check out an architect's or contractor's work in person; don't just rely on pictures. When interviewing references, ask past customers about work quality and promptness. Get at least three estimates and have a healthy distrust of the cheapest one, since the workmanship often isn't as good. Check with groups such as the Better Business Bureau before hiring anyone.

BE CLEAR

Make sure that you and your architect or contractor are in sync. If your goal is to restore historical items in the house, such as windows, doors, and floors, make sure that your architect understands and respects that approach and has access to artisans who can do the work well. State your budget, expectations, and the work you want done. If you decide to manage the contractor yourself, ask for a detailed price quote and provide a good set of drawings with specifications. Ask what materials will be used, such as underlayment, insulation, caulking, and paints, and find out if these are the best quality. Get a schedule with deadlines for specific tasks. Finally, get a warranty in writing (preferably in your contract) for the quality of the construction work.

SIGN A CONTRACT

Never hire anyone who refuses to put an agreement in writing. The American Institute of Architects (see Where to Find It, page 270) has contract templates that a homeowner can use for agreements with their architect and contractor. The Associated General Contractors of America recommends that a contractor's agreement include the contractor's name, address, and license number; architectural plans for the project, or a detailed description of the work; a statement that the work will be performed according to local codes and regulations; start and end dates; total costs and a payment schedule; warranties for workmanship and products; and a description of how change orders will be handled.

INVEST IN ESSENTIALS

Steven Harris, the Yale University architecture professor who designed Adam Gordon's town house renovation (see Bricks and Glass, page 253), advises that homeowners "do less,

but do it well." Says Harris, "To not fix the roof and paint everything instead is just not worth it—the roof will leak and destroy the house." He urges his clients to budget for essentials such as updated plumbing and electrical work before undertaking cosmetic changes. That said, he always tells his clients: "Before you start, consider every alternative you could ever want. If you want a fireman's pole running through three floors, like the one Adolf Loos designed for Josephine Baker's house in Paris, or an Olympic pool in the basement, like the one I installed in an 1840s town house in Manhattan, now is the time to put it out there, even if it is just to reject the idea. If you know today that you could add a thousand square feet to your house and you decide not to do it, that's a great decision. What you don't want is to say five years from now: I wish I had thought of that."

BE A GOOD CLIENT

Why has your contractor suddenly vanished? Could the reason be you? If you tend to stall making decisions or get in the way of the work, your team may lose patience. Designate one person to be the contact with the architect and contractor. Resolve differences with your partner so you do not give conflicting messages to your pros. If you notice problems during the renovation, go directly to the architect or contractor—don't take it up with the workers. If any aspect of the project needs to be modified midrenovation, put the change orders in writing and agree in advance on the work being done.

QUESTION LIST FOR ARCHITECTS AND CONTRACTORS

The following questions elaborate on the excellent checklist prepared by the Preservation Resource Center of New Orleans on what to ask before you hire anyone to renovate your historic home.

ASK THE ARCHITECT

1. Do you have experience with old buildings?

2. What is your design philosophy?

3. What services do you offer? Do the services include schematic design, working drawings, specification of materials, bidding and negotiations with contractors, and supervision of construction? If an architect is only needed for the preliminary phase of the project, will you agree to such an arrangement?

4. Are you knowledgeable about the requirements of city agencies?

5. Do you charge on a percentage of the construction costs, on an hourly basis, a flat fee, or a combination?

6. Do you use the standard AIA contract or another document?

7. Can you show me a portfolio of your work and supply references? Can I see your work in person?

8. When can you start? How long will each phase take?

9. Can I own the drawings that you produce for my project?

10. What are the challenges of my renovation?

11. Who from your firm will I be dealing with? Will the same person be designing the renovation?

12. How busy are you?

13. What is your track record with cost estimating?

ASK THE CONTRACTOR

1. Do you have experience with restorations?

2. Do you carry workmen's compensation and general liability insurance, and if so how much? Can your name be listed as additionally insured on liability and worker's compensation insurance? (This will protect you from claims from subcontractors or neighbors whose homes are damaged as a result of your renovation.)

3. Can you supply at least three references and refer me to previous work sites so that I can evaluate your work? (You can find out if the contractor has outstanding complaints filed against him or her by contacting your state's contractors' licensing board.)

4. Do you have a contractor's license from the city and state?

5. Can you supply credit references from suppliers, such as lumber stores, Sheetrock vendors, and others so I can be confident that you are financially solvent?

6. Are you comfortable working with architectural drawings and partnering with architects?

7. Are you skilled in getting a project through the permitting process?

8. Can you adapt to the draw schedule that my lender may dictate?

9. When can you start? How long will it take?

10. How many other projects do you have in progress? How often will you personally be on-site at my project?

WHERE TO FIND IT

A guide to professionals, artisans, and renovation sources.

THE FEDERALIST
James Mohn Design Studio
New York, NY
212-414-1477
www.jamesmohndesign.com

Stephan Jaklitsch Architects, PC
New York, NY
212-620-9166
www.sjaklitsch.com

CHARLESTON REVIVAL
Deborah Nevins & Associates
(landscape design)
212-925-1125
New York, NY
www.dnalandscape.com

G. P. Schafer Architect, PLLC
New York, NY
212-965-1355
www.gpschafer.com

Richard Marks Restorations, Inc.
Charleston, SC
843-853-0024

THE BRAHMIN
Heidi Pribell Interiors
Cambridge, MA
617-354-1445
www.heidipribell.com

FORGOTTEN GRANDEUR
Joseph V. Abbey (restoration consultant)
Troy, NY
518-274-6434

Zane Z. Studenroth Jr.
(decorative arts consultant)
Hudson, NY
518-671-6417

STAR TURN
Made LLC
Brooklyn, NY
718-834-0171
www.made-nyc.com

Sculpture House Casting
New York, NY
888-374-8665
www.sculptshop.com

THE NOSTALGIC
Kathryn Scott Design Studio
Brooklyn Heights, NY
718-935-0425
www.kathrynscott.com

STRAIGHT AND NARROW
Daniel E. Snyder, Architect, PC
Savannah, GA
912-238-0410
www.snyderarchitect.com

DIPLOMATIC CORE
Darryl Carter, Inc.
Washington, D.C.
202-234-5926
www.darrylcarter.com

SOUL SURVIVOR
Mariano Design
New York, NY
212-697-0219
www.marianodesign.net

CANADIAN GOTHIC
Grenier + Richards Architects
Montreal, Quebec
514-488-4054
www.gra1.ca

Scott Yetman Design
Montreal, Quebec
514-931-3389
www.scottyetman.com

SIMPLY FRENCH
Anne Attal Design
Brooklyn, NY
718-488-9634
anneattal@mac.com

Frank DeFalco (general contractor)
Brooklyn, NY
frankdefalco@mac.com

GHOST STORY
Arcanum Antiques and Interiors
Savannah, GA
912-236-6000
www.arcanumsavannah.com

ROCK 'N' ROLL REVIVAL
Miranda Brooks Landscape Design
New York, NY
212-228-3623
www.mirandabrooks.com

Lorraine Kirke (interior design)
LorrainekNY@aol.com

Live Load, Inc. (carpentry)
Thomas Muchowski
New York, NY
917-769-0151
www.liveloadbench.com

Richard H. Lewis, Architect
New York, NY
212-865-5661

Robert Padilla (decorative painting)
917-880-1818
www.latelierdesarts.com

ALL IN THE FAMILY
BDDW
New York, NY
212-625-1230
www.bddw.com

SKYLINE VIEW
Baxt/Ingui Architects PC
New York, NY
212-233-6740
www.baxtingui.com

Hamilton Design Associates
Brooklyn, NY
718-596-3200
www.hdanyc.com

MINIMALONIALISM
Minima
Philadelphia, PA
215-922-2002
www.minima.us

GRAPHIC POP
Bay City Builders, Inc. (general contractor)
William L. Lupton
Baltimore, MD
410-802-2112
www.lupton@verizon.net

Baltimore Finishing Works
(stripping and refinishing)
Baltimore, MD
410-235-7326

LIGHT BOX
Fernlund + Logan Architects
New York, NY
212-925-9628
www.fernlundlogan.com

BRICKS AND GLASS
Steven Harris Architects, LLP
New York, NY
212-587-1108
www.stevenharrisarchitects.com

BY PRODUCT

ARCHITECTURAL RESEARCH
www.ancestry.com (genealogy)

Digital Sanborn Maps
www.sanborn.umi.com

The Society of American Archivists
866-722-7858
www.archivists.org

ARCHITECTURAL SALVAGE
Al Bar-Wilmette Platers
(restoring hardware and metal fixtures)
Wilmette, IL
866-823-8404
www.albarwilmette.com

Chandelier Parts.com
Fergus Falls, MN
218-736-7000
www.chandelierparts.com

Gavin Historical Bricks
Iowa City, IA
319-354-5251
www.historicalbricks.com

Guide to Architectural Antiques and
Antique Lumber Companies
www.architecturalsalvagedirectory.com

Island Girl Salvage
Elk Grove Village, IL
847-593-2433
www.islandgirlsalvage.com

Keystone Antiques
Hudson, NY
518-822-1019
www.godmanskeystone.com

LooLoo Design (vintage bath and kitchen)
800-508-0022
www.looloodesign.com

Moon River Chattel
Brooklyn, NY
718-388-1121
www.moonriverchattel.com

Olde Good Things
(furniture, hardware, and odds and ends)
888-551-7333
www.oldegoodthings.com

Secondhand Rose
(vintage wallpaper and linoleum)
New York, NY
212-393-9002
www.secondhandrose.com

W. N. de Sherbinin Products, Inc. (lamp parts)
Danbury, CT
800-458-0010
www.wndesherbinin.com

Urban Archaeology
New York, NY
www.urbanarchaeology.com

Web Wilson (on-line auctions)
800-508-0022
www.webwilson.com

BROWNSTONE
Portland Brownstone Quarries
Portland, CT
860-342-2920
www.brownstonequarry.com

COLOR AND PAINT
Eve Ashcraft Studio
(architecture color consultation)
New York, NY
212-966-1506
www.eveashcraftstudio.com

Benjamin Moore
www.benjaminmoore.com

California Paints
800-225-1141
www.californiapaints.com

Colors of Historic Charleston
www.duron.com

Farrow & Ball
888-511-1121
www.farrow-ball.com

Fine Paints of Europe
800-332-1556
www.finepaintsofeurope.com

DECORATIVE PLASTER
Boston Ornament Company
617-787-4118
www.bostonornament.com

Decorators Supply Corporation
Chicago, IL
773-847-6300
www.decoratorssupply.com

Pure Plaster, Ltd. (artisanal plaster)
Jason Kuriloff
Brooklyn, NY
347-733-8363

FIREPLACES
Chimney Safety Institute of America
Plainfield, IN
317-837-5362
www.csia.org

Chimney Savers
Hillsborough, NJ
908-359-7798

Exhausto
770-587-3238
us.exhausto.com

Solid/Flue Chimney Systems
800-444-FLUE
www.solidflue.com

Stovax
www.stovax.com

GREEN BUILDING SUPPLIES
Bettencourt Green Building Supplies
Brooklyn, NY
800-883-7005
www.bettencourtwood.com

Build it Green! NYC
(recycled building materials)
Astoria, NY
718-777-0132
www.bignyc.org

Environmental Home Center
800-281-9785
www.environmentalhomecenter.com

HARDWARE
Architectural Grille (perforated grilles)
800-387-6267
archgrille.com

Baldwin
800-566-1986
www.baldwinhardware.com

E. R. Butler & Company
(reproduction hardware)
Boston and New York
www.erbutler.com

Liz's Antique Hardware
(antique and reproduction)
Los Angeles, CA
323-939-4403
www.lahardware.com

Merit (brass hardware and hinges)
Warrington, PA
215-343-2500
www.meritmetal.com

P.E. Guerin, Inc. (foundry and oldest
decorative hardware firm in the U.S.)
New York, NY
212-243-5270
www.peguerin.com

Whitechapel Ltd.
Jackson, NY
800-468-5534
www.whitechapel-ltd.com

LIGHTING
Circa Lighting
877-762-2323
www.circalighting.com

Rejuvenation
888-401-1900
www.rejuvenation.com

Schoolhouse Electric Co.
Portland, OR, and New York, NY
800-630-7113
www.schoolhouseelectric.com

MANTELS
Chesney's (reproduction)
New York, NY
646-840-0609
www.chesneys-usa.com

Francis J. Purcell (antique)
Philadelphia, PA
215-574-0700
www.francisjpurcell.com

Jamb (reproduction)
www.jamblimited.com

PLUMBING AND HEATING
Barber Wilsons & Co., Ltd.
www.barwil.co.uk

Bisque radiators
www.bisque.co.uk

STONE AND TILE
ABC Worldwide Stone
Westbury, NY
516-999-9412
www.abcworldwidestone.com

American Restoration Tile
(reproduction historic tile)
Mabelvale, AZ
501-455-1000
www.restorationtile.com

Rhodes Architectural Stone
(recycled antique stone)
Seattle, WA
206-709-3000
www.rhodes.org

WINDOWS
Architectural Windows and Entries
St. Peterburg, FL
800-747-6840
www.architecturalwindows.com

Bliss Nor-Am Doors & Windows Ltd.
315-469-3314
www.blissnoram.com

Zeluck Inc.
Brooklyn, NY
800-233-0101
www.zeluck.com

WOOD FLOORS
Antique & Vintage Woods of America, Ltd.
Pine Plains, NY
800-210-6704
www.antiqueandvintagewoods.com

Baba Fine Wood Floors
800-542-4812
www.baba.com

Carlisle Wide Plank Floors
Stoddard, NH
800-595-9663
www.wideplankflooring.com

Old Wood Workshop
Pomfret Center, CT
860-655-5259
www.oldwoodworkshop.com

WOODWORK
Park Slope Paint Strippers (wood restoration)
Dean Camenares
Brooklyn, NY
718-783-4112

ORGANIZATIONS

The American Institute of Architects
Washington, D.C.
800-AIA-3837
www.aia.org

The Associated General
Contractors of America
Arlington, VA
703-548-3118 (local)
800-242-1767 (publications)
www.agc.org

Institute of Classical Architecture &
Classical America
New York, NY
212-730-9646
www.classicist.org

New York Landmarks Conservancy
New York, NY
212-995-5260
www.nylandmarks.org

Preservation Resource Center of New Orleans
504-581-7032
www.prcno.org

GLOSSARY

ARCH: a curved construction that spans an opening.

ARCHITRAVE: in Classical architecture, the lowest portion of an entablature, the beam that spans from column to column and rests directly upon their capitals.

ARGON GAS: a colorless, odorless gas that when sandwiched between panes of Low-E glass improves a window's insulating qualities.

AWNING: a shading device, usually made of canvas, that is mounted on the outside of a door, window, or terrace.

BALUSTER: one of a series of short vertical posts used to support a stair handrail.

BALUSTRADE: a railing system composed of balusters and a top rail, as along the edge of a balcony.

BASEBOARD: an interior molding covering the joint of a wall and the adjoining floor.

BASEMENT: a floor of a building that is located partly or entirely below ground level. In a classic town house, the basement frequently contained kitchens and family dining and living rooms.

BAY: a regularly repeating division of a façade, marked by evenly spaced windows.

BAY WINDOW: a window or group of windows forming a bay in a room and projecting outward from the wall.

BOLECTION: a deep, unadorned molding, often found in paneling, doors, and fireplaces, which projects beyond the face of a panel or frame.

BRACKET: a projecting angled or curved form used as a wall support, such as to hold up balconies, lintels, pediments, and cornices.

BROWNSTONE: a dark brown or red brown sandstone, quarried and used for construction in the eastern United States during the nineteenth century. The term is also used to describe a dwelling sheathed in brown sandstone.

BUTT JOINT: a joint made by fastening two pieces of wood or other material together end to end.

BUTTER JOINT: in masonry, a fine quarter-inch mortar applied by hand between bricks.

CABINET: a case or cupboard usually having doors or shelves.

CAPITAL: the topmost member, usually decorated, of a column or pilaster.

CASEMENT: a window sash that is hinged on the side.

CELLAR: a type of basement, the term usually refers to a large underground room used for storage.

CEMENT TILE: colorful decorative tile, also known as encaustic, that originated in France and Belgium at the end of the nineteenth century.

CHAIR RAIL: a horizontal strip, usually wood, affixed to a plaster wall at a height that prevents the backs of chairs from damaging the wall surface.

CLAPBOARD: wood siding composed of horizontal, overlapping boards.

COFFERING: a ceiling with deeply recessed panels, often highly ornamental.

CONSOLE: a scroll-shaped decorative bracket.

CORBEL: a projecting stone that supports an overhanging weight.

CORNICE: a band, or molded projection, that tops a roof or wall.

COURSE: a horizontal row of bricks, shingles, stones, or other building material .

CREMONE BOLT: a type of hardware for locking French doors and windows.

CROWN: the top of an arch including the keystone.

DADO: the middle section of an ornamental paneling applied to the lower walls of a room above the baseboard.

DENTIL: small, square, toothlike blocks in a band underneath a cornice.

DOUBLE HUNG: window with two movable sashes that operate vertically. Double-hung sashes are held in an open position with the use of a coil spring block and balancing devices.

EGG AND DART: an ornamental band molding of egg forms alternating with dart forms.

ENGLISH BOND: brickwork with alternating headers and stretchers.

ENTABLATURE: a horizontal part in Classical architecture that rests on the columns and consists of architecture, frieze, and cornice.

EYEBROW WINDOW: a bottom-hinged, semicircular window, usually on the uppermost story of a house.

FACADE: the exterior face of a building, which serves as the architectural front.

FANLIGHT: a fixed window usually curved like a fan and positioned above a door.

FESTOON: a carved ornament in the form of a band, loop, or wreath; also called a garland or a swag.

FIRST-GROWTH LUMBER: wood taken from a forest that has never been logged or burned. See also: *old-growth wood.*

FLEMISH BOND: in brickwork, a pattern in which each course consists of headers and stretchers laid alternately.

FLUE: in a chimney, an incombustible and heat-resistant enclosed passage to vent a fireplace, furnace, or boiler to the outside air.

FORMSTONE: a faux-stone stucco veneer patented in Baltimore in the 1930s. The material was so popular in Baltimore for refacing row houses that one native—the film director John Waters—dubbed it "the polyester of brick."

FRENCH DOOR: a tall casement window that reaches to the floor, usually arranged in two leaves as a double door.

FRETWORK: ornamental openwork, often in a geometric pattern such as Greek key, in relief.

GARRET: the top story under the slope of a roof.

GLAZING: installing glass into windows and doors. Double-glazed refers to two panes of glass divided by a spacer and sealed together with dead air between the panes.

GRILLE: a decorative, openwork grating, usually of iron, used to protect a window door, or other opening.

GUTTER: a shallow channel of metal or wood set below and along the eaves of a building to catch and carry off rainwater from the roof.

GYPSUM: a common mineral consisting of hydrous calcium sulfate used in the making of plaster of Paris.

HARDWOOD: the wood of an angiospermous tree, as distinguished from that of a coniferous tree.

HEADER: a brick or stone laid in a wall so that its end is exposed.

HEART PINE: A rare southern hardwood cut from longleaf pine trees old enough to have developed heartwood. Known for its durability, handsome grain patterns, and warm red tones.

HEARTWOOD: the older, harder nonliving central wood of trees that is usually darker, denser, and more durable than the surrounding sapwood.

HERRINGBONE PATTERN: a way of assembling brick or wood in a diagonal zigzag fashion.

JAMB: the vertical posts that form the sides of a door or window frame, where the hinges are mounted.

JOIST: one of a series of parallel wood beams used to support floor and ceiling loads.

KEYSTONE: the central wedge-shaped section of a masonry arch.

LAMINATED GLASS: a safety glass consisting of two or more layers of glass, held together by an interlayer that holds together when shattered.

LIGHTS (OR LITES): individual panes of glass in a window or door.

LINTEL: a horizontal beam that spans a window or door opening and supports the wall above it (also known as a header).

LOW-E GLASS: low-emissivity glass coated with a thin layer of metal or metallic oxide to suppress radiative heat flow.

MANSARD: a roof having two slopes on all sides with the lower slope steeper than the upper one.

MANTEL: the beam or arch supporting the masonry above a fireplace.

MARQUETRY: decorative work in which elaborate patterns are formed by the insertion of pieces of a material such as wood or ivory into a common background.

MASONRY: brick, concrete, stone, or other materials bonded together with mortar to form walls and other solid construction.

MEDALLION: a decorative tablet or panel in a wall or ceiling bearing objects in relief, such as a figure, head, or flower.

MODILLIAN: ornamental blocks or brackets applied in series to a soffit, the underside of a cornice.

MOLDING: a decorative band or curved strip used for ornamentation or finishing.

MORTISE AND TENON: a joinery system in which two pieces of wood are attached by inserting the peg of one (the tenon) into a hole or groove (mortise) of the other, then glued or wedged into place.

MULLION: a vertical board that separates paired or multiple windows within a single opening.

MUNTIN: thin frames that separate paired or multiple windows within a single opening.

NICHE: a recess or hollow in a wall, usually for a statue or vase.

OLD-GROWTH WOOD: lumber taken from forests that are at least 200 years old. See also: *first-growth lumber.*

OVERMANTEL: an ornamental structure above a mantelpiece.

PANELING: a wall surface consisting of panels set within a framework of vertical stiles and horizontal rails.

PARQUET: a wood floor laid in a geometric pattern.

PICTURE RAIL: a molding installed along the top of a wall from which pictures can be hung from hooks.

PIER MIRROR: a tall, slender mirror often placed over pier tables between two windows to fill the narrow space and reflect light from the windows.

PLANK: a long, broad, and thick piece of sawed timber, usually two to four inches thick and at least eight inches wide.

PLASTER OF PARIS: a kind of plaster made of a white powdery substance consisting of hydrate of calcium sulphate, a quick-setting paste used chiefly for casts and molds.

PLAT BOOK: records, usually public and in book form, showing the location, size, and owner's name for each plot of land in a stated area.

POCKET DOOR: a door that slides into a hollow wall at the side of a doorway, eliminating the need for space for swinging doors.

POINTING, REPOINTING: the treatment of joints between bricks, stone, or other masonry by filling with mortar.

QUARTERSAWN: lumber sawed from quartered logs so that the annual rings are nearly at right angles to the wide face. Also referred to as tiger oak.

QUOIN: a structural form, usually of masonry, used at the corners of a building for the purpose of reinforcement.

ROW HOUSE: one of a series of houses connected by common sidewalls and forming a continuous group.

SASH: the framework that holds the glass in a window.

SEEDED GLASS: a bubble in glass that resembles a seed in shape or size.

SILL: the horizontal bottom member of a window or door opening.

SOLDIER COURSE: a row of bricks laid on end vertically, with the narrow side exposed in the face of the wall.

SOFTWOOD: lumber produced from coniferous trees such as pine and spruce.

STILE: vertical board that runs the full height of a sash, panel, or screen.

STRETCHER : a stone or brick laid horizontally with the long, narrow side exposed.

TONGUE AND GROOVE: a joint made by a tongue on one edge of a board fitting into a corresponding groove on the edge of another board.

TOWN HOUSE: a multistory urban house, attached or detached, that is built close to the street and scaled similarly to surrounding houses.

TRANSOM: a horizontal crossbar in a window, over a door, or between a door and a window. Transoms are often moveable for ventilation.

TRIPLE HUNG: a window, like those at Monticello, that has three movable sashes. Open to the floor, these windows adjust to varying breezes.

VALANCE: a short drapery or frame used as a decorative heading to conceal the top of curtains and fixtures.

WAINSCOT: a usually paneled wooden lining of an interior wall.

WEIGHT AND CHAIN: a weight-balance system used in the operation of single- or double-hung historic windows.

SUGGESTED READING

Belfoure, Charles, and Mary Ellen Hayward. *The Baltimore Rowhouse*. New York: Princeton Architectural Press, 2001.

Binney, Marcus. *Town Houses: Urban Houses from 1200 to the Present Day*. New York: Whitney Library of Design, 1998.

De Botton, Alain. *The Architecture of Happiness*. New York: Pantheon, 2006.

Garrett, Elisabeth Donaghy. *At Home: The American Family 1750–1870*. New York: Harry N. Abrams, 1990.

Gorlin, Alexander. *The New American Town House*. New York: Rizzoli, 2000.

Guild, Robin. *The Victorian House Book*. New York: Firefly Books, 2008.

Labine, Clem, and Carolyn Flaherty, eds. *The Old-House Journal Compendium*. New York: Overlook, 2007.

Lockwood, Charles. *Bricks and Brownstones: The New York Town House 1783–1929*. New York: Rizzoli, 2003.

Mumford, Lewis. *The Brown Decades: A Study of the Arts in America, 1865–1895*. New York: Dover, 1971.

Murphy, Kevin D. *The American Townhouse*. New York: Harry N. Abrams, 2005.

Shivers, Natalie. *Those Old Placid Rows: The Aesthetic and Development of the Baltimore Rowhouse*. Baltimore: Maclay & Associates, 1981.

Wharton, Edith, and Ogden Codman Jr. *The Decoration of Houses*. New York: Rizzoli, 2007.

ACKNOWLEDGMENTS

Our homes play a dual role in our lives, at once intimate and public. They are our private spheres, nurturing us and containing our secrets, while also serving as the means through which we share our lives with others. In creating this book, I was invited into the homes of many people, who all placed their confidence in me. For that privilege, and for the warm hospitality I received, I am most grateful. I am also indebted to the many talented architects, interior designers, and contractors who led me to the town houses documented here, and spent countless hours responding to my questions.

Brian Park, my partner on this project, is not only a wonderful photographer, but a terrific traveling companion, an unflappable and hard-working colleague, and a complete pleasure to be around. I am lucky to have Sarah Burnes as my agent as she is level-headed and wise and has become a trusted friend. Chris Pavone had the idea for this project and took a chance on me; I only regret not getting to know him better.

I owe so much to the top-notch team at Artisan. Ann Bramson inspires me daily with her warmth and perfect insights into making books better, including my own. Art director Jan Derevjanik was my sounding board throughout this project. I love her beautiful design, which was artfully created with the help of designer Stephanie Huntwork. Sigi Nacson, my smart and passionate editor, worked mightily to improve the manuscript and advocate for the book. Trent Duffy, Nancy Murray, Amy Corley, Erin Sainz, Suzanne Lander, Susan Baldaserini,

Barbara Peragine, and Quinn Rowan all assisted in so many ways. David Schiller's advice and enthusiasm was very much appreciated. Peter Workman is a publishing visionary and I feel privileged to have a book in his stable.

With photo shoots in ten cities, Brian and I collaborated with stylists from coast to coast. My wholehearted thanks to Laura Dotolo, Catherine Schneider, Amanda Betz, Joy Bruder, Natalie Evans, Susan Kessel, Julia Kininmonth, Bobbi Lin, Tara Monaghan, Geri Radin, and Kendra Smoot. Three of my favorite photographers—Paul Costello, Thibault Jeanson, and Jason Schmidt—were generous enough to allow me to use their photographs to fill in important gaps. The following firms kindly lent products or provided services: ABC Carpet & Home, Madeline Weinrib Atelier, John Robshaw, The Rug Company, The Stephen Williams House in Savannah, and Winston Flowers in Boston.

The advice of friends and colleagues was invaluable. Martha Maristany's suggestions on photography set the tone. Anne Johnson lent her unerring eye. Jennifer Rubell gave encouragement and sustenance. Marketing wiz Jessica Hundhausen proved a fine Southern hostess. My former colleagues at *House & Garden*, especially Dominique Browning and Betsy Pochoda, taught me how to look beyond the surface tell the story. I'm grateful to the editors who have more recently embraced my design journalism, including Margaret Russell, Pilar Guzmán, and Trish Hall.

The following people made valuable contributions: Erica Ackerberg, Eve Ashcraft, Sarah Bird, the Burnes family, Jill and John Bouratoglou, Sarah Crichton, Trent Farmer, Lucy Gilmour, Wendy Goodman, Susan Gross, Sarah Holbrooke, Eliza Honey, Fritz Karch, Cheryl Katz, Liz Kubany, Jonathan Lethem, Cristina Lindblad, David Mann, Trish Martin, Richard McGeehan, Jeffrey Miller, Betsy Nordlander, Joan Pope, Philip Reeser, Jen Renzi, Susan Ruhne, Mayer Rus, Leah Singer, Beverly Stanley, Judy Stanton, Kathleen and Charlie Tesnakis, and Madeline Weinrib. Clem Labine, founder of the *Old-House Journal* and all-around brownstone maven, was an important source of information on restoration, as was Alex Herrera at the New York Landmarks Conservancy.

Many, many thanks to my family: my parents, Arlene and Henry; my sister, Susan (who contributed incisive legal advice); my brother, Seth; my in-laws Marcia, Jerrold, and Barbara Simon; and my great-grandma, Martha Gardner. My husband, Joel Simon, inspires me daily, as do my sweet daughters Ruby and Lola, who have stood by me with love, enthusiasm, and infinite patience.

Finally, to the craftsmen who created these wonderful houses and the artisans who continue to maintain them; to homeowners and inhabitants of the homes, past and present; and to everyone who has struggled and cared enough to preserve them, I extend my deepest thanks.

INDEX